T0360483

Women, Work and Migration

This book looks at the migration and work experiences of six women who have migrated to Australia from China; Zimbabwe; South Korea; the United Kingdom; India and the Philippines. It sets their journeys out into three distinct periods of migration, including the first period of their lives when they reflect on their experiences growing up with their immediate families and the factors that encouraged them to gravitate towards a nursing career. The second period covers time when each of these women begin to think about where their career in nursing might take them. During this phase, these women take their first steps to leave their home country and migrate to Australia, often after several countries in-between. The final section allows the reader to understand how these women initially experience Australia when they first arrive and how they face challenges both personally and professionally after arrival in their new place they call home.

The discussions within these three sections cover both professional and personal/familial reflections, where differences in nursing identity between sending and destination country are discussed alongside the adjustments that the women needed to make to overcome loneliness and to successfully integrate into new organisational environments. Each chapter analyses migration as a life course, which considers why nurses leave their home country and find a new place to call home. Furthermore, if they find themselves thinking about returning to their country of birth; how or if they maintain transnational links, and how identity and ethnicity shape these responses.

These life trajectories are underscored by a historical context of nursing migration to Australia outlined in the opening chapter offering unique insights into the changing process of migration, accreditation, registration and settlement of nurses in Australia. The book will be of value to researchers, academics and students interested in gender studies, career and migration, health and nursing and international Human Resource Management (HRM).

Diane van den Broek is Associate Professor of Work and Organisational Studies at the University of Sydney Business School, Australia.

Dimitria Groutsis is Associate Professor of Work and Organisational Studies at the University of Sydney Business School, Australia.

Routledge Focus on Business and Management

The fields of business and management have grown exponentially as areas of research and education. This growth presents challenges for readers trying to keep up with the latest important insights. Routledge Focus on Business and Management presents small books on big topics and how they intersect with the world of business research.

Individually, each title in the series provides coverage of a key academic topic, whilst collectively, the series forms a comprehensive collection across the business disciplines.

Ephemeral Retailing
Pop-up Stores in a Postmodern Consumption Era
Ghalia Boustani

Effective Workforce Development
A Concise Guide for HR and Line Managers
Antonios Panagiotakopoulos

Employment Relations and Ethnic Minority Enterprise
An Ethnography of Chinese Restaurants in the UK
Xisi Li

Women, Work and Migration
Nursing in Australia
Diane van den Broek and Dimitria Groutsis

Distributed Leadership and Digital Innovation
The Argument for Couple Leadership
Caterina Maniscalco

For more information about this series, please visit: www.routledge.com/ Routledge-Focus-on-Business-and-Management/book-series/FBM

Women, Work and Migration
Nursing in Australia

Diane van den Broek and Dimitria Groutsis

Routledge
Taylor & Francis Group

NEW YORK AND LONDON

First published 2020
by Routledge
52 Vanderbilt Avenue, New York, NY 10017

and by Routledge
2 Park Square, Milton Park, Abingdon, Oxon, OX14 4RN

Routledge is an imprint of the Taylor & Francis Group, an informa business

© 2020 Taylor & Francis

The right of Diane van den Broek and Dimitria Groutsis to be identified as authors of this work has been asserted by them in accordance with sections 77 and 78 of the Copyright, Designs and Patents Act 1988.

All rights reserved. No part of this book may be reprinted or reproduced or utilised in any form or by any electronic, mechanical, or other means, now known or hereafter invented, including photocopying and recording, or in any information storage or retrieval system, without permission in writing from the publishers.

Trademark notice: Product or corporate names may be trademarks or registered trademarks, and are used only for identification and explanation without intent to infringe.

Library of Congress Cataloging-in-Publication Data
Names: Van den Broek, Diane, author. | Groutsis, Dimitria, author.
Title: Women, work and migration : nursing in Australia / Diane van den Broek and Dimitria Groutsis.
Description: New York : Routledge, 2019. | Series: Routledge focus on business and management | Includes bibliographical references and index.
Identifiers: LCCN 2019044817 | ISBN 9780367140649 (hardcover) | ISBN 9780429029967 (ebook)
Subjects: LCSH: Women foreign workers—Australia. | Women nurses—Australia—Social conditions. | Ethnopsychology—Australia. | Self-perception—Australia. | Transnationalism.
Classification: LCC HD6057.5.A8 V36 2019 | DDC 331.4/ 816107309269120994—dc23
LC record available at https://lccn.loc.gov/2019044817

ISBN: 978-0-367-14064-9 (hbk)
ISBN: 978-0-429-02996-7 (ebk)

Typeset in Times New Roman
by Apex CoVantage, LLC

Contents

Acknowledgements

This book is dedicated to nurses everywhere, and particularly to the six generous nurses who are represented in these pages. Also, we wish to thank our families respectively: Wayne, Ruth and Ellis Baker and John Mitchell.

Finally, we thank each other for our collaboration, including the debating and reflecting on the lives of these women over several years, and for those many researchers who by providing us their insights into nurse migration have made this journey all the more interesting.

1 Overview of the Book

Faces Behind the Numbers

Walk into any hospital in an Organisation for Economic Co-operation and Development (OECD) country and you will more than likely be cared for by a nurse who was born, or trained, overseas. In Australia for instance, overseas-qualified nurses have been a significant contributor to the health sector labour force for many decades. While this scenario has become very familiar to us; it is one which very few of us have given much detailed, or deep, thought to.

This book hopes to redirect attention to the many migrant women who work in our hospitals and care for our sick. It is designed to help develop a better understanding and appreciation of some of the factors that compel these women to leave their homeland and join a migrant healthcare workforce that takes them far away from their country of origin. It is designed to put a human face to the 'lived experience' of internationally mobile healthcare workers, a pattern of international mobility amongst this profession that has now reached unprecedented levels in terms of both size and the breadth of nations from which its constituents are drawn (WHO, 2018; Van Manen, 2016).

Although we focus on the stories of six female nurses who have migrated to Australia, their experiences may resonate with other migrant workers. The following pages reveal to us the people behind the statistics; they show us that migration is not an act undertaken lightly or something that, once done, is over and then forgotten. What emerges are stories of what initiates migration; what perpetuates ongoing migration; and how and why these transitions are undertaken. Through this we come to understand the dreams, aspirations and desires that shape these migrant women's decision to leave their homeland for work (Carling, 2001; De Haas, 2014). These experiences also have buried within them the ripple effects that all migration has on the personal lives of the migrant: their families; and their communities that are built and exist in both the country of origin and in the destination country.

We know that we are merely scratching the surface of the lives of the six women whose stories are recounted here. We do believe though, that what these women themselves reveal grants a valuable insight not only into their experience of migrating for work purposes, but also an insight into their professional dedication. We come to understand the challenges and fears they faced as they left their homeland to embark on new professional and personal challenges in a new country and a new workplace. The very simple proposition of this book rests on the contention that their experiences matter. They matter not only because the personal and professional experiences of all migrants tell us a lot about the country we live in and are a part of, but also because without their migration and their labour, our healthcare system would rapidly collapse.

With this in mind, we document the personal migration journeys of six women whose lives are in many ways ordinary, but whose experiences are in many other ways truly extraordinary. By being drawn into the twists and turns of these women's lives we are able to better understand the complex, but subtle and rarely spoken about, feelings that develop around migration, gender and care work. We are better able to see the process of the transformation that takes place when women leave home to pursue professional opportunities in a strikingly different country. By bringing together these stories we hope to provide a human account of global nursing migration: a story that complements existing material on healthcare migration. It hopes to minimise and counteract often reductionist and essentialist discussions about the need to fill 'skill gaps' and seeks to refute the sometimes ubiquitous, derogatory and xenophobic references to migrants as 'job-takers' and 'queue jumpers'.

Notwithstanding the significant migration flow after the turmoil of the Second World War, the issue of migration in Australia today has become a highly sensitive topic. World events, including the ascendance of anti-migration right-wing political agendas that incite fear-based and divisive rhetoric, policies and practices, particularly after the 9/11 tragedy, highlight the imperative to look at migration and migrant work in more nuanced ways. These events signal the need to understand migration and migrant workers not as a policy, or endless reserve supply lined up in a never-ending queue formed to undermine the opportunities of the local population, or as part of a deterministic push-pull migration explanation (Khoo et al., 2007; Kline, 2003). We were keen to understand, and highlight, how migrant workers contribute to positive change in this country through their hard labour. As with the local population, migrants have a strong and determined desire to contribute to this new country that they settle in, either temporarily or permanently while also having strong bonds to a country they have left behind. Many relate experiences that reflect the sense that they have one foot in the familial values, networks and traditions of the homeland they left behind, another foot embracing the new and unfamiliar land they have arrived into, as well as a third which might signal future aspirations. Taken together, this book hopes to further an understanding of the contradictory feelings of isolation, excitement and fear that these women experience when they embark on such an undertaking.

Faces Behind the Global Care Chain

The gendered nature of migration and work forms an important lens through which to understand the experience of the female overseas-qualified nurses who occupy the pages of this book. A gendered lens is critical to teasing out the different experiences of migration for men and women (Groutsis, 1998). While both migrate for similar reasons—for adventure, work, further education, for love, to name but a few of the reasons, the process and outcomes of migration and as such the experience of the migrant themselves is very much a gendered experience. For instance, migration policies have traditionally categorised the man as the head of the family unit, with the woman as the secondary entrant. As such, for many decades throughout the post-World War II period in Australia, migrant woman did not appear in migration statistics, as a skilled and qualified potential contributor to the Australian economy and labour force (Foster et al., 1991; Fincher et al., 1994; Vasta, 1992, 1993; see also Yeoh et al., 2002). Add to this, the more subtle yet powerful expectations, values and norms that are formed around gender in both sending and destination countries; and the evident power dynamics and imbalances these norms, values and expectations create, and we can see that the experience of migrant women is very different to that of migrant men. The labour market opportunities and outcomes for skilled migrants are also gendered. For instance, internationally, migrant women tend to be channelled into largely 'feminine' jobs: such as education, health, social work and the caring sectors (Carling, 2005; Piper, 2006; Yeates, 2009; Lutz, 2010).

As elaborated in Chapter 2, within Australia the highest representation of women working in any industry is in Health Care and Social Assistance, at 78.1% and over 90% of the nursing workforce are women (AIHW, 2016; WGEA, 2015). Looking globally the picture is also highly gendered. Women make up around 42% of the estimated global paid working population and within the health sector, in many countries they comprise over 75% of the workforce, making them indispensable as contributors to the delivery of health care services. The World Health Organisation (WHO) estimate that nurses and midwives represent nearly 50% of the global health workforce. They also estimate that there will be a need for nine million additional nurses by 2030, particularly in countries in Southeast Asia and Africa (WHO, 2018).

While these continents have a desperate need for basic health care infrastructure, it is high income countries such as the UK, Canada, the US and Australia that continue to be the primary recipients and benefactors of migrant nurses (Connell, 2010; Kingma, 2007). In contrast, low-income countries' demand for health services will continue to outstrip supply, due to the increased workforce shortages which result from nurses migrating to high income countries. (Liu et al., 2017). Ironically, the source countries of nurses migrating to Australia are the very regions that need them most.

Notwithstanding the documented need for nurses globally, the heavy demand for overseas-trained nurses from developing and middle-income countries to developed countries can be traced back to the post-World War II period (Groutsis, 1998). Over the decades since the 1950s, the demands of wealthy and aged populations with the increased engagement of domestic care has led to the emergence of a 'global care chain' which has shaped and strengthened global links between paid and unpaid care work (Hochschild, 2000; Yeates, 2004; Kofman and Raghuram, 2012). These transnational arrangements highlight that it is women who meet the demand for care work in both the unpaid and paid domains. They reflect disparities in wealth and opportunity between countries; welfare regimes that shape familial relations, and regulatory regimes that shape migration patterns.

Care arrangements tie countries into 'global circuits of care in distinctive ways and have different kinds of care provisioning and histories of gendered migrations' (Kofman and Raghuram, 2012, 408). Within high income countries like Australia, the heavy reliance on overseas-qualified nurses is illustrated by workforce projections that point to a near 30% shortfall in nursing staff by 2025 (Australian Institute of Health and Welfare, 2012). In times past, the source countries most likely would have included the UK and Ireland, however these countries are now more likely to be points of destination rather than points of origin. For some decades now, nurses migrating to work in countries like Australia are just as likely to migrate from countries such as India, China, Zimbabwe, the Philippines and South Africa, as well as the UK and Ireland (Hawthorne, 2007; Ohr et al., 2009; Iredale, 2012; Groutsis and van den Broek, 2014).

Often the nurses who do choose to migrate do so on the basis of prevailing fluctuations in government regulation and labour market supply and demand conditions. Consequently, the countries nurses migrate to may represent their second or even third destination choice rather than their first. Many migrants may use a country as a stepping-stone to another. Others plan to arrive at their destination country to settle permanently. Others still see it as a short-term event in their career life cycle, to develop their skills or to send back remittances.

The varied motivators surrounding the migration context, which has been well observed by a wealth of research—explored further on, affords us some understanding of the many challenges and opportunities that nurses face when they migrate. What is largely absent from the existing literature however, is a direct and personal focus on the experiences of the women who have managed those threats and embraced those opportunities; and for this reason above all others it is the stories of the women themselves, in their own voices, rather than the statistics that underlie them, who are the main focus of this book.

While the women whose stories unfold here, reflect the rich multicultural diversity of the Australian migrant nursing workforce, there are also some important high-income countries that are not represented here, notably Ireland. However, the six countries that are represented in this book highlight the regions where migrant nurses are often drawn from to support the Australian health sector. Some aspects of these women's lives are unique and intimate to their own experiences of work and migration. Unlike some other migrants, these six women did not vocalise a motivation to migrate due to war, personal harm from persecution or to avoid overt dangerous political turmoil. They did however articulate that they left their country in search of new lives. Whether this shift would be temporary or permanent at the time of their decision to migrate was not known, a point which highlights the lack of linearity in the process of migration. In many cases it was a future life unknown. But in all cases, it was a future work life based on nursing. The critical shortages that existed in the global nursing workforce was therefore a vital passport to this new life.

The Approach of This Book

To date there have been numerous books and articles that chronicle nurse migration: among them, Choy's book on Filipino nurses (2010) and George's study of Indian nurses (2005), which focused on particular ethnic groups of migrant nurses. There is also a wealth of research that we will build on in the next chapter, that develops an understanding about the nature and link between migration, gender and nursing work.

In the subsequent chapters we then present six biographical chapters, each devoted to the individual experience of migrant nurses. Each of the six nurses begins their story by describing their upbringing, their family and the community in which they grew up. Each discusses the expectations and dreams they had as a young woman embarking on a life and a career in nursing; each reflects on a transition into adulthood and how this was influenced by their gender, their class, their culture and family circumstances; and each explores the avenues they pursued and the obstacles they encountered in making their way around the world, using the nursing profession as their ticket to work internationally.

What becomes especially clear as we read their stories is how critical junctures and relationships shaped their experiences and their decisions, which often involved various twists and turns based often on serendipity, unimaginable barriers and subsequent opportunities: pre- and post-migration. There is a case to argue that these barriers and opportunities may not be unique to these particular women, or to those working in the nursing profession more broadly; but there is also a case to argue that these experiences have a commonality about the vulnerability and challenges that this hyper-mobile career can bring.

It should be noted that rather than following an explicit theoretical approach, this book builds on several themes that relate to career, professional identity, migration, ethnicity and gender. It does not seek to provide an overtly academic account of nursing work, women and migration. It is intended to appeal not just to students and academics but to others, such as nurse practitioners, keen to develop an understanding of the experiences of migrant women nurses 'up close'.

The book adopts a phenomenological tone, one that might be loosely summarised by the question: "How would you describe your experiences?" In taking this approach we aim to bring out the 'lived experience' of nursing work, rather than on theorising its role in contemporary global (gendered) migration. Writing this book through a lived experience is designed to encourage a reflection on what it means to 'live a life' as we *live it rather than how we might conceptualise it*. What this means is that the book purposefully focuses on the individual and the personal which takes precedence over the broader political, economic and labour-market standpoints that traditionally dominate analyses of global migration. Our hope is that this approach will allow readers to better grasp how migration is lived and to recognise that while we might have a strong view on migration, these views may be based on limited knowledge of how and why migration decisions are made and how we ultimately benefit from these decisions each time we walk into our local hospital (Van Manen, 1984, 2016; Mapedzahama et al., 2012).

Therefore, in placing nurses' own voices at the very heart of this book we hope that we can allow others to reflect on the experiences of those who toil in one of the most dynamic, yet poorly paid and undervalued, professions, while at the same time noting the strong sense of professional identity, altruism and care. Hearing the voices of these women allow us to understanding how these women adjust to, and manage migration and how they negotiate new, unfamiliar and often unsupported work contexts. It also allows us to reflect as a nation on what migrant workers contribute to the fabric of our society.

The approach in this book provides an opportunity to appreciate how nurse's agency and career mobility will vary, along with their respective ability to migrate with some measure of discretion in terms of opportunities offered in their countries of origin and destination (Tams and Arthur, 2010; Xu and Zhang, 2005). As we will see, one nurse might choose to migrate to fulfil a desire for a temporary working holiday in a foreign country; while another will leave with no intention of returning, discouraged by poor employment and career prospects in their country of origin or difficult political or economic circumstances. The specific variables that prompt migration differ enormously (Buchan et al., 2004, 2005).

Collecting and Analysing Our Interviews

We first made contact with the participants in this book indirectly. This contact was achieved through the help of professional associations and the nursing union, public and private hospitals and migrant resource centres. Ethical protocols governing qualitative research such as this meant that we required a willingness of women to participate in the research, and we did not seek information from anyone who did not agree to these ethical protocols. We subsequently identified six overseas-qualified nurses from different countries who represented a variety of clinical roles in both public and private hospitals in Australia.

An initial meeting was held with each nurse to discuss the project and gain their consent to be included in these pages. This was followed by several interviews, conducted at either the participant's workplace or their home. Most participants took part in two or three interviews, each lasting several hours, and all agreed to have their photograph taken to be included in the book.

Throughout this research we used an open-ended interview style to ensure as much as possible that we could better understand our participant's experiences and that these experiences were represented as respectfully as they could be. This open-ended approach was intended, to some extent, to allow each nurse to take the conversation in any direction that they thought was important to them. We were keen to avoid the use of set interview questions, rather focusing on broader themes to support discussion and reflection: allowing the participant's story to unfold as naturally and freely as possible.

The background to these stories involved several key phases which is reflected in the presentation and structure of the book. While we drew on Everett S. Lee's seminal work to shape the keynote phases of migration: being 'there', being ' in-between' and being 'here' (Lee, 1966), we note and emphasise the non-linear process of migration. Indeed, we do not infer a clear chronology in these themes but use these as markers to frame the fluid and dynamic experience of migration for these women. We also intersect these themes with important cross-cutting factors as we examine their desires and expectations in leaving their country of origin to work abroad (Lee, 1966; see also Cohen, 1996).

For example, being 'there' recognised these women's early years growing up and draws upon familial or community and country traditions that shape one's expectations, dreams and future possibilities. This period revolves around recollections and reflections of formative years in one's country of origin, focusing on early childhood and adulthood, as well as ethnicity, gender, class, family, friends, education and neighbourhood in early, but foundational years. During this period the discussion focused on how these women reflected on their upbringing, their place within their family, expectations and dreams of where they saw career, and often where others expected them to be. Recalling these years often raised feelings of uncertainty, potential opportunity and a nascent yearning for significant change about the personal and professional possibilities that the future might have delivered.

Being 'in-between' refers to the period when these women left their homeland. It is a period of transition in life when experimentation and the prospect of alternate possibilities about potential lives and careers is at the forefront of one's decision-making. Being 'in-between' reflects their first experience of migration—the intervening stages—as Lee notes. This theme reflects a gradual realisation that leaving one's homeland was front of mind and important for personal and professional growth. It is during this stage that the women we talk to dig deeper into their personal reflections about their motivation to leave their home country, and how a nursing career might provide an opportunity to do so. In many ways these stages are stepping-stones on what might be an ongoing mobility to yet further locations. As Chapter 2 elaborates, this phase also highlights how the quality of advice: provided by an elaborate network of intermediaries we call the migration industry, including recruiters and migration agents, shapes the realisation of dreams. In many ways, this is the first stage in an ongoing, and at times unsettling, migration process.

Being 'here' should not be read as a period of time which designates a final destination, but rather as the time we call 'the present'. As such, this represents a designation of time when our discussions take place, which reflect experiences of career position and a moment in time when these women are settled in Australia. Therefore, being 'here' does not denote the finality of locating in Australia as an end point, but rather marks the present. As such, discussion covered recent experiences in Australia, focusing on their search for meaningful work and secure and stable personal circumstances. Discussions also included the potential and or the need to (re)invent one's professional identity in a new country context. It also entailed an understanding of the way in which ties with the destination country might change over time and how isolation from that past might deepen, while new possibilities, beginnings, hopes and desires might also eventuate.

Together, these phases are as much about how institutions and organisations regulate and shape nurse migration as they are about how individual choices shape migration. Therefore, while we know that migrant work is regulated by visa or professional accreditation and status, personal plans and aspirations are rarely predetermined and individual agency, cultural and familial influence are often opportunistic, tenuous and highly variable. What is clear is that while these women migrated from different countries under wildly different political, economic and social circumstances, there are also commonalities between them. Our role as researchers in their story is also important to recognise.

Reflexivity

Undertaking multiple interviews with the women in this book allowed us to piece together a rich picture of how and why they chose to train in the nursing profession and how these choices influenced their migration decisions. We wanted to understand what it meant to be a nurse—and, moreover a woman, and a migrant nurse—in an everyday 'lived' sense, including why they were drawn into the profession. Given our indisputable power to interpret these stories, particularly our freedom to prioritise and/or omit interview material, we do not claim these interviews amounted to the 'absolute truth' of these women's lives. Any interview is highly contextual and, as such, serves as an arena for social interaction and construction rather than a chance to gather 'objective' data (Alvesson, 2003, 169). In the process we recognised our responsibility to ensure the integrity of each nurse whose story is recounted here and to faithfully represent our discussions with each nurse to our readers. Accordingly, we sought to act as our interviewee's advocates while at the same time helping readers to understand how 'major societal shifts might be experienced through individual perspectives' (Oakley, 2010, 426; Omeri and Atkins, 2002).

Moreover, as researchers, we are aware of the importance of integrity and trust when undertaking our research. We must not only attempt to ensure the integrity of each nurse whose story is recounted here, but also to reflect on how we influence data collection and analysis. As qualitative researchers, we understand our privileged position as researchers who shape the collection, selection, and interpretation of data and the co-construction processes that occur between the research participants and the researcher (Callaway, 1992; Finlay, 2002; Bell et al., 2018). As Hertz (1997) states, such reflexivity involves the need for researchers to have 'an ongoing conversation about the experience while simultaneously living in the moment' (p. viii). Therefore, although we cannot claim to fully understand (or fully represent) the lived experience of each woman in these pages because we have not experienced what they have, we do possess an awareness about the issues we discuss. As women who trained professionally in the fields of history and political economy, and also as children of immigrants we did recognise some shared understanding with the women in this book. While these factors helped us to become involved in a reflexive dialogue during different stages of the research process, we also recognise how our own individual responses to interviews shaped the text in the following chapters.

Final Note

Finally, the reason we wanted to write this book was because we were keen to contribute to a broader conversation about the nation in which we live and work. We were keen to bring the conversation about migration back to the hearts of migrants and to the heart of a nation. As such, we were keen to ground the migration stories of these women within the social, cultural and economic relations embedded within Australian society (Castles, 2010).

Australia is a country that has been built on migration. However, the pattern of migration has, since the late 1990s, shifted from one based on family reunion to one based on demand-driven skilled migration. Despite changes to the types of migration, much of the prosperity that this country enjoys, particularly throughout the post-World War II period, has been based on the contribution of migrant labour. Yet we know very little about those individuals who have contributed to this prosperity.

Migration is a process that is experienced individually. It is an ongoing personal journey, regardless of the degree, or absence of any strategic or explicit planning involved. Migration is a process that continues over the span of a life course. It involves processes that build and rebuild the present and the future. It also links into, and is set within, wider processes of, in this case, global (and gendered) health care mobility.

We wrote this book because, while we had read about, and researched, nurse migration for some years, we were keen to provide migrant nurses a broader platform from which to tell their own life stories. We wanted to share their everyday, and often hidden experiences with a wider audience to understand the opportunities they took advantage of, the opportunities they chose not to pursue, and the opportunities they felt were denied them. Above all, we wanted to bring intimate and personal stories which help us also to reflect on our own place within this country.

The approach of this book proved an ideal means of juxtaposing the experiences of nurses who have grown up in six diverse national contexts, including: Korea, Zimbabwe, China, India, the United Kingdon, and the Philippines. The experiences of these women highlight the commonalities that unite many female migrant nurses who pursue dreams that improve their own lives but also the lives of their families who seek advancement in new and unfamiliar nations. The stories recounted here are stories of hope, anticipation and also escape.

We know that the six women in this book have shown great bravery in discussing their anticipations, anxieties about the choices that they have made and their fear of being accepted and respected in their professions and their social world. These fears and anxieties tell us a lot about the collective migration story both in Australia and overseas, which is embedded in an important socio-political and economic context. Their stories help us to comprehend modern migration 'from below': that is, from a personal perspective. We hope that these accounts add to important conversations about the significant dignified contribution that migrant workers make to this and other countries around the world. As such, we thank the six women featured in this book for their generosity, their honesty and their willingness to allow us to recount their experiences in the following pages.

References

ABS. (2015). *Gender Composition of the Workforce: By Industry*. Labour Force, Australia, Detailed, Quarterly, February 2015, cat. no. 6291.0.55.003. www.abs. gov.au/ausstats/abs@.nsf/mf/6291.0.55.003. Accessed 6.11.19.

Alvesson, M. (2003). Methodology for close up studies: Struggling with closeness and closure. *Higher Education*, 46, 167–193.

Australian Institute of Health and Welfare. (2016). Nursing and midwifery workforce 2015. Cat. no. WEB 141. Canberra: AIHW. Viewed 27 October 2019, https://www.aihw.gov.au/reports/workforce/nursing-and-midwifery-workforce-2015

Bell, E., Bryman, A., and Harley, B. (2018). *Business Research Methods*. Oxford: Oxford University Press.

Buchan, J., Jobanputra, R., Gough, P., and Hutt, R. (2005). *Internationally Recruited Nurses in London: Profile and Implications for Policy*. King's Fund Working Paper, London, September.

Buchan, J., Parkin, T., and Sochalski, J. (2004). *International Nurse Mobility: Trends and Policy Implications*. Geneva: World Health Organisation, ICN and RCN.

Callaway, H. (1992). Ethnography and experience: Gender implications in fieldwork and texts. In J. Okely and H. Callaway (Eds.), *Anthropology and Autobiography* (pp. 29–49). New York: Routledge Chapman Hall.

Carling, J. (2001). *Aspiration and Ability in International Migration: Cape Verdean Experiences of Mobility and Immobility*. Master's Thesis, University of Oslo, Oslo.

Carling, J. (2005). Gender dimensions of international migration. *Global Migration Perspectives*, 35, 1–26.

Castles, S. (2010). Understanding global migration: A social transformation perspective. *Journal of Ethnic and Migration Studies*, 36(10), 1565–1586.

Choy, C. (2010). Nurses across borders: Foregrounding international migration in nursing history. *Nursing History Review*, 18, 12–28.

Cohen, R. (1996). *Theories of migration*. Cheltenham: Edward Elgar.

Connell, J. (2010). *Migration and the Globalisation of Health Care*. Cheltenham: Edward Elgar.

De Haas, H. (2014). *Migration Theory: Quo Vadas?* International Migration Institute, Working Paper Series, Paper 100, November.

Everett, S. L. and Lee, E. S. (1966). A theory of migration. *Demography*, 3(1), 47–57.

Fincher, R., Foster, L., and Wilmot, R. (1994). *Gender, Equity and Australian Immigration Policy*. Canberra: Bureau of Immigration and Population Research.

Finlay, L. (2002). "Outing" the researcher: The provenance, process, and practice of reflexivity. *Qualitative Health Research*, 12(4), 531–545.

Foster, L., Marshall, A., and Williams, F. (1991). *Discrimination Against Immigrant Workers in Australia*. Canberra: AGPS.

George Sheba, M. (2005). *When Women Come First: Gender and Class in Transnational Migration*, Berkeley: University of California Press.

Groutsis, D. (1998). *Snakes and Ladders, Overseas Qualified Immigrant Women in the Australian Labour Market: The Case of Overseas Trained Doctors and Nurses*. PhD Thesis, UNSW, Australia.

Groutsis, D. and van den Broek, D. (2014). *Importing Skills and Diversity Management: The Case of Migrant Nurses*. Emerging Health Policy Research Conference, Menzies Centre for Health Policy, University of Sydney and Australian National University, October.

Hawthorne, L. (2007). *The Impact of Globalisation on Medical and Nursing Workforce Supply-Policy, Accreditation and Labour Market Integration Issues for Canada and Australia*. Presentation at University of Toronto, March.

Hertz, R. (1997). *Reflexivity & Voice*. Sage Publications, CA.

Hochschild, A. (2000). Global care chains and emotional surplus value. In W. Hutton and A. Giddens (Eds.), *On the Edge: Living with Global Capitalism*. London: Johnathon Cape.

Iredale, R. R. (2012). Major issues in the global mobility of health professionals. In S. D. Short and F. McDonald (Eds.), *Health Workforce Governance* (pp. 15–40). Farnham, UK: Ashgate.

Khoo, S. E., Voigt-Graf, C., McDonald, P., & Hugo, G. (2007). Temporary Skilled Migration to Australia: Employers' Perspectives1. *International Migration*, 45(4), 175–201.

Kingma, M. (2006). *Nurses on the Move: Migration and the Global Health Care Economy*. Ithaca, NY: Cornell University Press

Kline, D. S. (2003). Push and pull factors in international nurse migration. *Journal of Nursing Scholarship*, 35(2), 107–111.

Kofman, E. and Raghuram, P. (2012). Women, migration, and care: Explorations of diversity and dynamism in the global South. *Social Politics*, 19(3), 408–432.

Liu, J. X., Goryakin, Y., Maeda, A., Bruckner, T., and Scheffler, R. (2017). Global health workforce labor market projections for 2030. *Human Resources for Health*, 15(1), 11.

Lutz, H. (2010). Gender in the migratory process. *Journal of Ethnic and Migration Studies*, 36(10), 1647–1663.

Mapedzahama, V., Rudge, T., West, S., and Perron, A. (2012). Black nurse in white space? Rethinking the in/visibility of race within the Australian nursing workplace. *Nursing Inquiry*, 19(2), 153–164.

Oakley, A. (2010). The social science of biographical life-writing: Some methodological and ethical issues. *International Journal of Social Research Methodology*, 13(5), 425–439.

Ohr, S. O., Parker, V., Jeong, S., and Joyce, T. (2009). Migration of nurses in Australia: Where and why? *Australian Journal of Primary Health*, 16(1), 17–24.

Omeri, A. and Atkins, K. (2002). Lived experiences of immigrant nurses in New South Wales, Australia: Searching for meaning. *International Journal of Nursing Studies*, 39(5), 495–505.

Piper, N. (2006). Gendering the politics of migration 1. *International Migration Review*, 40(1), 133–164.

Tams, S. and Arthur, M. B. (2010). New directions for boundaryless careers: Agency and interdependence in a changing world. *Journal of Organizational Behavior*, 31(5), 629–646.

Van Manen, M. (1984). *Doing Phenomenological Research and Writing: An Introduction* (Monograph 7: Curriculum Praxis Monograph Series). Canada: University of Alberta, Department of Education.

Van Manen, M. (2016). *Researching Lived Experience: Human Science for an Action Sensitive Pedagogy*. Abingdon: Routledge.

Vasta, E. (1992). *Immigrant Women and the Politics of Resistance*. Paper presented at the Conference, The Politics of Speaking Out: Immigrant Women Ten Years On, Immigrant Women's Speakout Association, October.

Vasta, E. (1993). Immigrant women and the politics of resistance. *Australian Feminist Studies*, 8(18), 5–23.

Workplace Gender Equality Agency. (2015). *Gender Composition of the Workforce: By Industry*. www.wgea.gov.au. Accessed 6.1.19.

World Health Organization. (2018). www.who.int/mediacentre/factsheets/nursing-midwifery/en/

Xu, Y. and Zhang, J. (2005). One size doesn't fit all: Ethics of international nurse recruitment from the conceptual framework of Stakeholder Interests. *Nurse Ethics*, 12, 571–581.

Yeates, N. (2004). A dialogue with "global care chain" analysis: Nurse migration in the Irish context. *Feminist Review*, 77, 79–95.

Yeates, N. (2009). *Globalizing Care Economies and Migrant Workers: Explorations in Global Care Chains*. Basingstoke, UK: Palgrave Macmillan.

Yeoh, B. S., Graham, E., & Boyle, P. J. (2002). Migrations and family relations in the Asia Pacific region. *Asian and Pacific Migration Journal*, 11(1), 1–11.

2 Migration, Gender and Nursing Care Work

Introduction

Interdependencies between gender, migration and care have been well established in a diverse array of literature. This chapter outlines the context-specific and locally sensitive nature of nurse migration. It focuses on the factors that inform these women's decision to leave their countries: in particular how the state, and the market actively shape migration processes. The chapter also highlights common circumstances that bind the migration experience, which help to explain the circumstances of the lives of the migrant nurses in this book. This includes the way that professional and gender identity intertwines to shape participation within global care systems. What also unifies the stories of these migrant nurses is the timing of their participation in this distinct period of Australian, and the world's, health migration history.

Changing Patterns of Contemporary Migration in Australia: The Rise of Skilled, Temporary and Demand-Driven Migration

As intimated earlier, Australian mass migration in the immediate post-war period was predominantly sourced from the UK and Ireland, and various source countries in continental Europe, followed by the Middle East and South America from the 1970s. From the 1980s onwards the major source regions changed significantly with settler arrivals from the Asian region making up an increasing share of immigrants. For instance, in 1977 the UK and Ireland still comprised the largest group of immigrants settling in Australia (28%), with the Asian region making up a relatively smaller proportion of total arrivals (15%). By 1985 the tide of change had begun with immigrants from the UK and Ireland comprising 16%, and the Asian region 40% of total settler arrivals (DIEA, 1986; DIEA, 1988).

By the mid-1990s the major immigration source continued to be the Asian region, accounting for 32% of total settler arrivals—with 20% from the Southeast Asian region and 12% from the Northeast Asian region. By the new millennium the pattern of migration from Asia continued and by 2010 the Asian region was the most dominant source of migrants into Australia (ABS, 2017).

The shift in the migrant source countries and a declining need for the 'factory fodder' of the 1950s and 1960s generated a shift from predominantly unskilled migrant labour (Alcorso, 1989; Vasta, 1993; Collins, 1988; Lever-Tracy and Quinlan, 1988) to the immigration of skilled labour, especially since the 1980s (Alcorso, 1995; BIPR, 1990; Borowski and Shu, 1992, 32; Chapman and Iredale, 1990; Iredale, 2001). Between 1980 and 1990 there was a 90% increase in skilled migration, including the arrival of business migrants, temporary specialists and technicians: a period which resulted in the beginning of temporary labour migration. Skilled migration increased as a proportion of the migration programme since 1984/85 when it accounted for 13% of total migrants. The proportion of skilled migrants rose to 30% in 1993/94 (Fincher et al., 1994; Young and Madden, 1992; BIPR, 1994). By the turn of the first decade of the new millennium 62% of residents with engineering degrees were born overseas, 57% of information technology professionals, 53% of accountants, 47% of doctors, and 29% of nurses, compared to 26% of the total population (Hawthorne, 2015, S174).

In addition to the type of migrant and the source countries of migration Australian migration regulations have also fostered a change in the migrant entering Australia. Since the late 1990s the focus has shifted from 'settler' migration and family reunion to demand-driven and employer-sponsored migration (Wright et al., 2017). This trend has consolidated the influence of non-state agencies, including recruitment and migration agents, employers, independent contractors and educational institutions, as principal managing agents of the migration of international labour, particularly throughout the OECD (Groutsis et al., 2015; OECD, 2012). Notably, the change in the pattern of migration and the regulations underscoring it have allowed Australian employers (including the public health authorities) to efficiently and swiftly address significant shortfalls in nurses and midwives needed to meet the challenges of our increasingly aging and growing population (Wellard and Stockhausen, 2010, 8; Connell, 2010).

While this book argues that migrants themselves are active agents in their mobility, the state plays a crucial role in shaping immigration through migration policy and through the policies around skills accreditation and labour market entry (Groutsis, 2003). As mentioned in the previous chapter, there has been a heavy reliance on migration to meet the workforce requirements of the health sector, particularly in rural and regional areas of Australia (Groutsis, 2006). Statistics tell us that while the global demand for nurses is not new, what is new is the profile of the countries from which nurses are migrating. For example, since the 1950s the stereotypical migrant nurse working in Australia would most likely have migrated from New Zealand, the UK or Ireland. Since the 1970s however, nurses are increasingly migrating from developing countries such as Zimbabwe, China and India. We know that there will be a need for some nine million additional nurses by 2030, with countries such as the UK, Canada, the US and Australia being the primary recipients and benefactors of migrant nurses (WHO, 2018; Connell, 2010; Hawthorne, 2015). Within Australian hospitals today, nurses from Australia, England, Scotland and Ireland are very likely to be working alongside a highly ethnically diverse group of nurses.

Circular migration has also become a more common phenomenon, alongside temporary skilled migration patterns, in many developed economies (Vertovec, 2007; Hawthorne, 2005; Iredale, 2001; Skeldon, 2012; Agunias and Newland, 2007). Given the nature of transnationalism, many skilled migrants are born and raised in one country, perhaps educated in several others, and gain employment and utilise their hard-earned skills to leverage employment in a wider range of countries. This means that many migrants, including nurses, might move between several countries rather than settling in any one location. For example, around 40% of newly registered nurses working in Ireland between 2000 and 2009 were from outside the European Union and were then re-recruited by Australia, Canada and the United States (US) (Health Workforce Australia, 2014, 11).

Within Australia the various nurse migration pathways have varied across a spectrum of General Skilled Migration, Employer Nomination Schemes; Regional Sponsored Migration Schemes; and Student Visa schemes. As already mentioned, nurses from China, India, Zimbabwe and the Philippines are particularly attracted through the Student visa and the Temporary Work (Skilled) Visa (Subclass 457) replaced in 2018, by the Temporary Skill Shortage (Subclass 482). We can see similar migration patterns internationally with Britain attracting largely Caribbean nurses, and the US attracting Filipino nurses through temporary skilled migration schemes (Department of Immigration and Citizenship, 2009; World Health Organisation; Cheniza Choy, 2010; Stasiulis and Bakan, 2003, 107; Ball, 2004).

Many of the women we will read about in this book migrated with the support of their home governments. Indeed, many governments, particularly the governments of China, Korea and the Philippines, have explicitly educated and trained nurses to export these skills to meet global skills shortages and attract remittances back to home countries (Bach, 2010; Connell, 2010). In countries like the Philippines for instance, these contributions are significant. For example, in 2011, eight-and-a-half million overseas Filipino workers and two million emigrants remitted around $20 billion (accounting for 10% of GDP) to the Philippine economy (Prescott and Nichter, 2014,

118). Evidently, women are particularly fruitful 'exports' due to the amount and frequency of remittances that they send to their country of origin with research showing that they send a higher proportion of their income and send money more regularly and for longer periods of time than their male migrant counterparts (IOM, 2010). Moreover, while female-led migration is numerically smaller than male-led migration, migrant women are more likely to 'maintain their emotional concerns and advice from afar, sustaining an active, though distant, transnational mothering' (Kofman and Raghuram, 2012, 417).

Breaking the Barriers: Qualifications, Accreditation and Migration Intermediaries

With the emergence of mass-migration throughout the post-war period, the registration process played a direct and indirect role in limiting and facilitating the access of overseas-qualified nurses into the Australian healthcare sector.

The establishment of a recognised minimum standard came with the rise of the Australasian Trained Nurses Association (ATNA) in 1899. Regulating standards throughout Australia with a growing population, posed an unwieldy task for a single national body, highlighting the need to devolve such responsibilities. Although state branches developed soon after the establishment of ATNA, it was not until 1933 that all states were officially given the responsibility of regulating nursing training and monitoring minimum standards of nursing practice (Katz et al., 1976: 12).

The introduction of state registration boards began in 1920 with the establishment of the South Australian board. The New South Wales (NSW) Registration Board—established in 1924—followed soon after. The devolution of the registration responsibilities to the states resulted in diverse standards throughout Australia. Consequently, national mobility was restricted for nurses seeking work in other states. This has since changed with the establishment of a central agency: the Australian Health Practitioner Regulation Agency (AHPRA). AHPRA is a centralised national agency through which overseas-trained nurses must first report in order to gain qualifications assessment and registration (www.ahpra.gov.au/).

Throughout the history of qualifications accreditation and registration of overseas-qualified nurses, there has been a clear distinction made between those arriving from English-speaking countries compared with those from non-English-speaking countries. For those from English-speaking countries, registration was strictly a procedural matter, requiring an acknowledgement of paper documentation, while the ANAC examination was by-passed (ANAC, 1983). In contrast, for those from non-English-speaking countries, exams, bridging courses and an English language assessment have combined to create the process of accreditation and registration. Throughout the 1990s and into the new millennium the focus of qualifications accreditation has turned to a competency-based approach.

The reforms were part of the redefinition of the nursing profession. The female dominance in nursing provided a perfect test case for the recognition of the skills women brought to the workplace. These skills had in the past been overlooked as 'innate', and kept nursing in a subordinate position in the health sector. The gendered nature of tasks undertaken was analysed and featured in the language defining the skills and competencies central to the training and registration process (Parkes, 1992, 20). Also, the competency-based approach held the potential to include the unique skills that overseas-qualified professionals brought to the occupation. This was possible due to the potential shift from a recognition of qualifications to a recognition of skills.

While we have alluded to the importance of migration regulations and demand-driven migration, it is important to note the significant presence of the labour market conditions underscoring the entry of overseas-qualified nurses. Throughout Australia's post-war history of migration we can safely say that the accreditation and registration process has been tightened and relaxed based on labour market demand conditions. In more recent years, the more flexible arrangements to entry have played into these demand-driven arrangements adding further complexity to the process of migration and by association, labour market entry.

As we hear from the nurses later, irrespective of whether they arrived on a student, permanent or temporary sponsored visa, many viewed their employment and residency in Australia as a potentially long-term aspiration. This desire is important to acknowledge because nurses often access temporary and sponsored migration as a pathway to gain direct entry into a job within Australia that is relatively commensurate to pre-migration skills and qualifications. For instance, for nurses entering Australia under the general skilled migration scheme, the ability to secure a job may be more unpredictable and riskier, as compared with securing a position through an employer sponsorship arrangement. Therefore, sponsored nurses can effectively fast-track what can often be outdated qualification assessments (Hawthorne, 2015, S174).

By 2012, English language ability had become the key criterion for skilled migrant selection in Australia, along with qualification level and employer sponsorship (Hawthorne, 2015, S182). In all cases however as mentioned, registration and accreditation are prerequisites and often extremely costly aspects of nurse migration, particularly for nurses from non-English-speaking countries who must progress through a more complex process of qualifications accreditation. The Australian Nursing and Midwifery Accreditation Council's (ANMAC) International Services section also assesses the skills of nurses and midwives seeking to migrate to Australia to assess if an applicant's nursing qualifications are suitable for permanent migration. Many of the nurses we get to know in this book, were required to complete expensive bridging programmes offered through professional or educational institutions in order to attain employment at similar levels to those they were working at in their home countries.

There are other complexities related to the actual migration process that are also often forgotten, or less evident to onlookers. Mobility requires the assistance of migration intermediaries that charge a fee for service to supply anything from personal loans, transportation services, housing advice as well as negotiating employment contracts and assistance with visa documentation (Goss and Lindquist, 1995; Coe et al., 2010). International nurse migration has risen to unprecedented levels and is now a multibillion-dollar global industry as international recruitment firms become much more targeted in how they create and manage the supply and demand of nurses to employers and to educational institutions around the world. Governments and employers can now pay recruitment agents up to $10,000 for each skilled migrant worker placed in jobs in Europe and the US (Gammeltoft-Hansen and Sorensen, 2013, 9).

While some of these intermediaries may be based on familiar family and trust networks, this does not necessarily mean that they are. For example, there are numerous examples of co-ethnic exploitation where migrants place trust in recruiters or migration agents with which they are familiar through family connections or in their home countries where the trust is then abused by migration intermediary actors who charge a fee for services. As such, dichotomies between (less trusting) commercial and (more trusting) familial intermediaries may be less apparent than assumed (Tilly, 2007; Ryan et al., 2008; Anderson, 2010; de Haas, 2010; Velayuthum, 2013; van den Broek and Groutsis, 2017).

Therefore while 'decisions to migrate are often made within a larger context of gendered interactions and expectations between individuals and within families and institutions' (Donato et al., 2006, 6; Mahler and Pessar, 2006), heavily gendered migration networks also reflect the intermediaries that facilitate that process (van den Broek, Harvey and Groutsis, 2016; Donato et al., 2006, 12).

While developing a clear picture of intermediary activities is difficult, we know that the women in this book undertook quite complex and often daunting logistical processes in order to migrate. Indeed, the variation in the quality of services provided can often be a crucial factor that shapes a nurse's ability to control their location within the labour market (Salt and Stein, 1997; Agunias and Newland, 2007; Sporton, 2013; Groutsis et al., 2015). For instance, media reports, such as this one in the New York Times in 1998, reported that hundreds of nurses had been illegally smuggled into the US from the Philippines and South Korea by an illegal ring that capitalised on nursing shortages within the US health system. Smuggling networks, involving 'professional' workers meant that in this case, the migrants were not hiding beneath blankets in trucks, or circumventing 'legal' passage on 'leaky boats' but rather were transported on commercial airlines using illegal and counterfeit documentation. These nurses paid their intermediaries fees between US$1,500 to US$7,500 to attain visas to work in the US, and rather than earning the local wage of $14 an hour, were employed as nurses' aides and paid as little as US$5 an hour (Seelye, 1998). These stories and reports show that migration intermediaries are crucial stakeholders in the migration experience, playing a significant role in providing opportunities but also in overcoming barriers to seamless migration.

With the Cap in Hand: Gender and Professional Identity

As with all professions, nursing attracts a certain type of person. Many of the women we spoke to in this book, and many others we have read about, express a desire early on in their lives to care for people. They often have a family history in similar fields and they also seek security in their career choice (Duffield et al., 2004). Altruistic reasons and a desire to help others are often the primary motivation to seek out nursing as a career (Duffield et al., [insert date], 466). A career in nursing is akin to a calling, which reflects a deep desire to devote oneself to serving people according to the high values of the task or profession (Raatikainen, 1997). This call to help and care for others might have been a life-long dream or it may have been a desire to help others later in life (Beck, 2000). This motivation could also explain the expanse of literature analysing the issues nurses face (and their potential exit from the industry) when patient care is compromised through rationalised healthcare systems; impossible workloads and poor peer relations; as well as the inability to provide good care that can lead to a burden of guilt and overcommitment (Buchanan and Considine, 2002; Hall and Kiesners, 2005).

As suggested above, there is also much evidence that nurses are attracted into the profession because of the security and the mobility that nursing affords through the 'exchange of cultures, expertise and opportunity that enriches nursing and societies everywhere' (Trant and Usher, 2010). There are multiple and strong reasons why nurses leave their homeland to pursue new dreams in unfamiliar countries (Buchan et al., 2004; Bourgeault et al., 2010). For example, nurses who migrate from countries such as India, Pakistan and Mauritius migrate to the UK to gain professional and personal advancement that may not be immediately available in their homeland. By contrast, nurses migrating from the UK, Australia, New Zealand, Ireland or the US tend to migrate for personal or lifestyle reasons, rather than purely professional motivations (Buchan et al., 2005, 8–9). As such, economic and political instability and insecurity, educational and/or career opportunities and family reasons are to varying degrees all important motivators for nurses to migrate (Bourgeault et al., 2010, 33).

However, there are also other important factors at play here. Much like the national profile of employed Australian nurses, most migrant nurses are female, representing over 90% of the nursing workforce (AIHW, 2016; WGEA, 2015). Looking globally, the picture is also highly gendered. Women make up around 42% of the estimated global paid working population and within the health sector in many countries they comprise over 70% of the workforce, making them indispensable as contributors to the delivery of health care services (WHO, 2018).

Hochschild's (2000) notion of the 'global care chain' encapsulates how women support the bulk of care work not only in their home countries but around the world, undertaking a wide range of important paid and unpaid care work (Yeates, 2004, 2009; Lutz, 2008; Ehrenreich and Hochschild, 2003; Parreñas, 2001). Care work, like nursing, has highlighted particular challenges, especially where welfare regimes and familial relations differ between countries (i.e. the way child and elder care is commodified and health/hospital infrastructure). Here, we see the 'complex causal relations that tie together migration, gendered labour and care regimes' (Kofman and Raghura, 2012, 409).

Nursing as a profession has been an important, and well-documented part of care work (Buchan et al., 2004; Winkelmann-Gleed, 2006; Connell, 2010; Hawthorne, 2005; Bourgeault et al., 2012; Kingma, 2006). Drawing on the wealth of existing research on nurse migration, including George (2005); Kingma (2006); Choy (2003); Ryan (2007); Connell (2010) and van den Broek and Groutsis (2017), we know that nurses have always been hyper-mobile, as reflected in the often-cited marketing slogan used by the American Nurses Association in the 1960s that 'Your cap is your passport' (Kingma, 2006, 23). Of course, nurse mobility is not just driven by the state. For example, when nurses use their cap as their passport, they become interconnected occupationally, professionally and also emotionally. The dynamism of the profession and the continuity of this mobility has combined with the gendered and emotional nature of nursing work which helps to bind a strong occupational standing and unique field of expertise (van Maanen and Barley, 1984, 314; Abbott and Meerabeau, 1998).

The experiences of particular ethnic groups of nurses have also been discussed. For example, Catherine Ceniza Choy (2006) explored the history of

Filipino nurse migration to the US, particularly focusing on the racialised, gendered and classed transnational nature of the labour force within the context of the US colonial presence in the Philippines. Heavily influenced by the Americanised hospital training system operating in the Philippines, nurses migrated in huge numbers during the American colonial rule in the early twentieth century, a pattern which continues to this day.

Similarly, George's (2005) work into the migration of nurses from the Indian state of Kerala to the US as single or married women outlined the difficulties nurses experienced in integrating into American work and life as well as the difficulties their husbands had in adjusting to their new (sometimes inferior) social role and social status. Her work highlighted how institutions, such as the church, became a pivotal institution in the identity building and integration process that took place for Indian nurses and their families. The book helps us to recognise the role that gender identity, family and spiritual institutions play for some of the women we talk to here and feeds into an understanding of the significant reconfigurations around gender and class relations that can take place both for male and female migrants. These works have helped to build a clearer understanding about how nurses renegotiate around very contrasting national cultures and traditions.

As part of a majority white ethnic group, Ryan also highlights how Irish nurses occupied an ambiguous position as European insiders, but cultural outsiders, as they migrated to the UK for work. Again, the multilayered and shifting dynamics and intersections of gender, location and occupational status impacted heavily on their experiences and their sense of Irish identity. The potential emotional loneliness and isolation that comes from being part of transnational families with specific expectations of and obligations to parents, spouses and children, are also particularly acute for many of these migrant nurses, irrespective of where they have migrated from (Ryan, 2007).

These books, and countless journal articles, based on nurses and nursing as a profession, have provided invaluable research into various aspects of nurse migration. They are part of a wider tradition of books that recognise the importance of adopting a detailed biographical approach to understanding the nature of work and the experiences of workers. During his lifetime, Studs Terkel brought the world of work to readers by understanding what work meant for workers under a variety of different circumstances. His book, *Working*, (1974) highlights that for many, work combines contradictory elements of extreme mundanity and (at times) existential depth and satisfaction. More recently in *Nice Work* (2010), Jana Wendt follows the day-to-day working lives of anthropologists, artists, managers, priests and boxers. When we become aware of these workers' various daily routines, we can better understand what de Botton (2010) has encapsulated as 'The

Pleasures and Sorrows of Work'. The contradictions, the pleasures and pain, and above all, the necessity to labour are all discussed in de Botton's work.

These books remind us of the centrality of work to many of our lives. They help us to get closer to understanding the challenges and joys that different types of workers experience as they toil in various types of occupations. We rarely take the opportunity to ponder this activity that is so central to all our lives. De Botton suggests that we find it difficult to reflect on our working lives 'properly' because most of us work in jobs that were often chosen for us 'by our sixteen-year-old selves' or by parental and/or community pressure (de Botton, 2010). This may or may not be so in all cases, but there are also common attributes here that relate to how work, and the search for meaningful work has a meaning 'well over and beyond the reward of the paycheck' (Terkel, 1974, 14).

Despite the unique features of nurse mobility and despite the fact that over 30% of nurses working in Australia were born overseas and just under 20% of these nurses were born in India, Malaysia and China (AIHW, 2012), we know surprisingly little about their individual joys and sorrows of migration. As echoed elsewhere, we need more 'human level' research to advance our understanding of what global mobility actually means on an emotional level (Favell et al., 2007).

Nurse migration is a more sophisticated industry than it has ever been in the past. Going back to the early colonial missionary activities of the nineteenth century, nurses, including figures such as Florence Nightingale, often eschewed their comfortable urban environment to work in far-flung and relatively challenging colonial outposts. Conversely, a flood of nurses now travels in the opposite direction, away from countries in need of health services to those that can offer professional and personal opportunities. Therefore, it is also worth noting that when nurses leave their home countries 'they also create care gaps . . . (h)ence, care demands are both being created and met through women's employment' (Kofman and Raghuram, 2012, 409).

While we in Australia reap the benefit of a relatively well-resourced health sector, the brain drain caused by nurse migration is significant. Agencies such as the World Health Organisation, the Organisation for Economic Co-operation and Development and the International Labor Organization have highlighted that the most acute nurse shortages are often found in the lower-income countries where health services can often be life-threatening. This 'brain drain' of health care workers has particularly disadvantaged some African and Southeast Asian countries. For example, Southeast Asia, which bears 30% of the global disease burden, has only 10% of the global health workforce, but contributes thousands of health workers to the global labour pool (IOM, 2006).

In an attempt to reduce the negative impact of the brain drain in 2004 the World Health Assembly (WHA) requested the WHO develop a code of practice on the international recruitment of health workers. After a global consultation process, a World Health Organization Code of Practice on International Recruitment of Health Personnel for Better Management of Health Worker Migration established an agreed set of ethical standards for recruitment of overseas health care workers which was adopted by the WHA in May 2010, (WHO, 2010). However, a recent report from the WHO secretariat shows a very poor uptake of the code concluding that there is a need to invest more effort in involving stakeholders at a national level and in improving data collection and sharing (Edge and Hoffman, 2013). Global regulatory bodies like the International Council of Nurses also provide important informational resources that support the development of professional infrastructure and education for nurses.

Once situated and working in Australia, another challenge facing migrant nurses is integrating smoothly into their workplace or living situation. Sometimes viewed as 'outsiders' or as a transient stock of labour, rather than as potentially long-term committed members of the local nursing workforce, challenges from both migrants and their co-workers can develop very quickly. At a professional level, there can be a perception by individuals and organisations, including the government, employers and unions (as well as the local nurse colleagues) that migrant nurses are less trained and/or transient. In some cases there is evidence that overt or more subtle discrimination and racism pose considerable difficulties for migrant nurses (Abood and Schinella, 1995; Omeri and Atkins, 2002; Xu, 2007; Mapedzahama et al., 2012).

Conclusion

The attraction and management of migrant nurses employed in countries like Australia, Ireland, the US, Canada, the UK and the Gulf countries has developed into a mature industry. While there are myriad reasons why nurses choose to migrate, one important motivator is the desire for greater opportunities for their nursing career and for the future of their families both in Australia and overseas. It is these dreams that we want to highlight in the remaining chapters. Therefore, while it is important to understand the context in which these women migrate, their personal stories are the main focus of this book.

This book depends on the nurses' own accounts of their work and their migration. However, to understand these processes, it is also necessary to have some reference points that situate the work and migration context in which these nurses live and work. It is necessary to develop an understanding of the sociopolitical and nurse migration context of the period in which these nurses were, and are, living. The discussion developed here was not intended as an expansive and comprehensive review of nurse migration or gender and professional identity, however, it presents an important context from which to understand and reference each of the journeys undertaken by the women who tell their stories here.

As de Botton (rather bleakly) suggests, many of us rarely reflect in detail on our working lives because these activities may often seem mundane and uninteresting. However, it becomes clear how important a nursing career was for many of these women from a very early age. Nursing provided these women with the opportunity to secure work overseas and to advance professionally (Connell, 2010, 94).

While work is no doubt an important necessity in all of our lives, this should not dispel an interest and a curiosity about our relationships to our own work and our understanding of others' relationship to their work. Neither should it dispel an interest and a curiosity about the wider political, economic and social context in which our career and migration choices are made. Indeed, exploring the personal circumstances of these women's lives helps us to better understand the nature of their professional achievements and, along with the local nurses they work with, fully grasp our reliance on them and the indebtedness we have to them as they toil in Australian hospitals each day.

However, these nurses' professional experiences are also overladen with individual and personal aspiration and hope. They share a profound desire for change and to experience liberty and love, to find a place where opportunity might, on the face of it, seem boundless. It is these dreams that we hope are conveyed in the following chapters.

References

Abbott, P. and Meerabeau, L. (Eds.). (1998). *The Sociology of the Caring Professions*. Psychology Press.

Abood, P. and Schinella, A. (1995). Culture, racism and sexuality. *Infocus Ethnic Communities' Council of NSW Inc.*, 18(5), September–October.

Agunias, D. (2009). *Guiding the Invisible Hand: Making Migration Intermediaries Work for Development*. Human Development Research Paper, 22.

Agunias, D. R. and Newland, K. (2007). *Circular Migration and Development: Trends, Policy Routes, and Ways Forward*. Migration Policy Institute Policy Brief, Washington, April 2007.

Alcorso, C. (1989). *Newly Arrived Immigrant Women in the Workforce*. Report for the Office of Multicultural Affairs, Centre for Multicultural Studies, University of Wollongong, Wollongong.

Anderson, B. (2010). Migration, immigration controls and the fashioning of precarious workers. *Work, employment and society*, 24(2), 300–317.

Australian Bureau of Statistics (ABS). (2017). *Census of Population and Housing: Reflecting Australia—Stories from the Census, 2016*. ABS Publication No. 2071.0, Canberra.

Australian Institute of Health and Welfare (AIHW). (2012). *Nursing and Midwifery Workforce 2011*. National Health Workforce Series Number 2, Cat. no. HWL 48. Canberra: AIHW.

Australian Institute of Health and Welfare (AIHW). (2016). *Nursing and midwifery workforce 2015*. www.aihw.gov.au/reports/workforce/nursing-and-midwifery-workforce-2015/data

Australian Nursing Assessment Council (ANAC). (1983). *First Annual Report*. Committee on Professional Qualifications, Canberra.

Bach, S. (2010). Managed migration? Nurse recruitment and the consequences of state policy. *Industrial Relations Journal*, 41(3), 249–266.

Ball, R. (2004). Divergent development, racialized rights: Globalized labour markets and the trade of nurses: The case of the Philippines. *Women's Studies International Forum*, 27, 119–133.

Beck, C. T. (2000). The experience of choosing nursing as a career. *Journal of Nursing Education*, 39(7), 320–322.

Borowski, A and Shu, J (1992) Australia's Population Trends and Prospects, 1991, AGPS, Canberra.

Bourgeault, I., Neiterman, E., LeBrun, J., Viers, K., and Winkup, J. (2010). *Brain Gain, Drain and Waste: The Experiences of Internationally Educated Health Professionals in Canada*. CIHR/Health Canada.

Bourgeault, I. L., Sutherns, R., MacDonald, M., & Luce, J. (2012). Problematising public and private work spaces: midwives' work in hospitals and in homes. *Midwifery*, 28(5), 582–590.

Buchan, J., Jobanputra, R., Gough, P., and Hutt, R. (2005). *Internationally Recruited Nurses in London: Profile and Implications for Policy*. King's Fund Working Paper, London, September.

Buchan, J., Parkin, T., and Sochalski, J. (2004). *International Nurse Mobility: Trends and Policy Implications*. Geneva: World Health Organisation, ICN and RCN.

Buchanan, J. and Considine, G. (2002). *Stop Telling Us to Cope!: NSW Nurses Explain Why They Are Leaving the Profession*. Australian Centre for Industrial Relations Research and Training.

Bureau of Immigration and Population Research (BIPR). (1994). *Bureau of Immigration and Population Research Bulletin*, Issue no. 12, October 1994.

Chapman, B. J., & Iredale, R. R. (1993). Immigrant qualifications: Recognition and relative wage outcomes. *International Migration Review*, 27(2), 359–387.

Choy, C. (2010). Nurses across borders: Foregrounding international migration in nursing history. *Nursing History Review*, 18, 12–28.

Choy, C. C. (2003). *Empire of care: Nursing and migration in Filipino American history*. Duke University Press.

Coe, N. M., Jones, K., and Ward, K. (2010). The business of temporary staffing: A developing research agenda. *Geography Compass*, 4(8), 1055–1068.

Collins, J. (1988). *Migrant Hands in a Distant Land, Australia's Post-War Immigration*. 1st Edition. Sydney: Pluto Press.

Connell, J. (2010). *Migration and the Globalisation of Health Care*. Cheltenham: Edward Elgar.

de Botton, A. (2010). *The Pleasures and Sorrows of Work*. London: Penguin UK.

de Haas, H. (2010). *Migration transitions*. International Migration Institute.

Department of Immigration and Citizenship. (2009). www.immi.gov.au/media/statistics/pef/457-stats-state-territory-june09.pdf. Accessed 20.6.11.

Department of Immigration Local Government and Ethnic Affairs. (1986). *Australia's Population Trends and Prospects*. Canberra: AGPS.

Department of Immigration Local Government and Ethnic Affairs. (1988). *Asia's Statistical Note No. 36*. Canberra: AGPS.

Duffield, C., Pallas, L. O. B., and Aitken, L. M. (2004). Nurses who work outside nursing. *Journal of Advanced Nursing*, 47(6), 664–671.

Edge, J. S., & Hoffman, S. J. (2013). Empirical impact evaluation of the WHO Global Code of Practice on the International Recruitment of Health Personnel in Australia, Canada, UK and USA. *Globalization and Health, 9*(1), 60.

Ehrenreich, B. and Hochschild, A. R. (2003). *Global Woman: Nannies, Maids, and Sex Workers in the New Economy*. New York: Macmillan.

Favell, A., Feldblum, M., and Smith, M. P. (2007). The human face of global mobility: A research agenda. *Society, 44*(2), 15–25.

Fincher, R., Foster, L. E., and Wilmot, R. (1994). *Gender Equity and Australian Immigration Policy*. Canberra: Australian Government Pub. Service.

Gammeltoft-Hansen, T. and Sorensen, N. N. (Eds.). (2013). *The Migration Industry and the Commercialization of International Migration*. Abingdon: Routledge.

George, S. M. (2005). *When Women COME first: Gender and Class in Transnational Migration*. Berkeley: University of California Press.

Goss, J. and Lindquist, B. (1995). Conceptualizing international labor migration: A structuration perspective. *International Migration Review*, 317–351.

Groutsis, D. (2003). The state, immigration policy and labour market practices: The case of overseas-trained doctors. *Journal of Industrial Relations*, 45(1), 67–86.

Groutsis, D. (2006). Geography and credentialism: The assessment and accreditation of overseas-trained doctors. *Health Sociology Review*, 15(1), 59–70.

Groutsis, D., van den Broek, D., and Harvey, W. S. (2015). Transformations in network governance: The case of migration intermediaries. *Journal of Ethnic and Migration Studies*, 41(10), 1558–1576.

Hall, L. M. and Kiesners, D. (2005). A narrative approach to understanding the nursing work environment in Canada. *Social Science & Medicine*, 61(12), 2482–2491.

Hawthorne, L. (2005). Picking winners: The recent transformation of Australia's skill migration policy. *International Migration Review*, 39, 663–696.

Hawthorne, L. (2015). The impact of skilled migration on foreign qualification recognition reform in Australia. *Canadian Public Policy*, 41, S173–S187.

Health Workforce Australia. (2014). *Immigration in Focus 2014*. Australia's Health Workforce Series. file:///E:/Research%20projects/Migration 457%20 visa/Literature/ REPORTS%20DATA/Health%20workforce%20data%202013.pdf

Hochschild, A. R. (2000). Global care chains and emotional surplus value. In W. Hutton and A. Giddens (Eds.), *On the Edge: Living with Global Capitalism*. London: Jonathan Cape.

International Organisation for Migration. (2006). *Migration and Human Resources for Health: From Awareness to Action*. International Dialogue on Migration.

International Organisation for Migration. (2010). *World Migration Report 2010: The Future of Migration—Building Capacity for Change*. Geneva: International Organization for Migration.

Iredale, R. (2001). The migration of professionals: Theories and typologies. *International Migration*, 39(5), 7–26.

Katz, F. M., Mathers, K., Pepe, T., and White, R. H. (1976). *Stepping Out: Nurses and their New Roles*. Kensington, Australia: NSW University Press.

Kanaiaupuni, S. M. (2000). Reframing the migration question: An analysis of men, women, and gender in Mexico. *Social forces*, 78(4), 1311–1347.

Kingma, M. (2006). *Nurses on the Move: Migration and the Global Health Care Economy*. Ithaca: Cornell University Press.

Lever-Tracy, C. and Quinlan, M. (1988). *A Divided Working Class: Ethnic Segmentation and Industrial Conflict in Australia*. London and New York: Routledge and Kegan Paul.

Lutz H. (2008). *Migration and domestic work: a European perspective on a global theme*. Aldershot: Ashgate Publishing.

Mahler, S. J., & Pessar, P. R. (2006). Gender matters: Ethnographers bring gender from the periphery toward the core of migration studies. *International migration review*, 40(1), 27–63.

Mapedzahama, V., Rudge, T., West, S., and Perron, A. (2012). Black nurse in white space? Rethinking the in/visibility of race within the Australian nursing workplace. *Nursing Inquiry*, 19(2), 153–164.

OECD. (2012). *Harnessing the Skills of Migrants and Diasporas to Foster Development: Policy Options*. French Ministry of Foreign Affairs, France.

Omeri, A. and Atkins, K. (2002). Lived experiences of immigrant nurses in New South Wales, Australia: Searching for meaning. *International Journal of Nursing Studies*, 39, 495–505.

Parkes, R. (1992, December/January). Nursing competencies. Applying a competency based training system to nursing. Part one: Entry to EN and RN practice. *The Australian Nurses Journal*, 21(6), 7–8.

Parreñas, R. S. (2001). *Servants of Globalization: Women, Migration and Domestic Work*. Palo Alto: Stanford University Press.

Prescott, M. and Nichter, M. (2014). Transnational nurse migration: Future directions for medical anthropological research. *Social Science & Medicine*, 107, 113–123.

Raatikainen, R. (1997). Nursing care as a calling. *Journal of Advanced Nursing*, 25(6), 1111–1115.

Ryan, L. (2007). Migrant women, social networks and motherhood: The experiences of Irish nurses in Britain. *Sociology*, 41(2), 295–312.

Ryan, L., Sales, R., Tilki, M., & Siara, B. (2008). Social networks, social support and social capital: The experiences of recent Polish migrants in London. *Sociology*, 42(4), 672–690.

Salt, J. and Stein, J. (1997). Migration as a business: The case of trafficking. *International Migration*, 35(4), 467–494.

Seelye, K. (1998). U.S. strikes at smuggling ring that exploited foreign nurses. *New York Times*, January 15. www.nytimes.com/1998/01/15/us/us-strikes-at-smuggling-ring-that-exploited-foreign-nurses.html

Skeldon, R. (2012). Going round in circles: Circular migration, poverty alleviation and marginality. *International Migration*, 50(3), 43–60.

Sporton, D. (2013). "They control my life": The role of local recruitment agencies in East European migration to the UK. *Population, Space and Place*, 19(5), 443–458.

Stasiulis, D. K. and Bakan, A. (2003). *Negotiating Citizenship: Migrant Women in Canada and the Global System*. Basingstoke: Palgrave.

Terkel, S. (1974). *Working: People Talk About What They Do All Day and How They Feel About What They Do*. New York: Pantheon/Random House

Tilly, C. (2007, March). Trust networks in transnational migration. In *Sociological forum* (Vol. 22, No. 1, pp. 3–24). Oxford, UK: Blackwell Publishing Ltd.

Trant, K. and Usher, S. (Eds.). (2010). *Nurse: Past, Present and Future: The Making of Modern Nursing*. Black Dog.

van den Broek, D. and Groutsis, D. (2017). Global nursing and the lived experience of migration intermediaries. *Work, Employment and Society*, 31(5), 851–860.

van den Broek, D., Harvey, W., and Groutsis, D. (2016). Commercial migration intermediaries and the segmentation of skilled migrant employment. *Work, Employment and Society*, 30(3), 523–534.

Van Maanen, J. and Barley, S. R. (1984). Occupational communities: Culture and control in organizations. *Research in Organisational Behaviour* 6: 287–365.

Velayutham, S. (2013). Precarious experiences of Indians in Australia on 457 temporary work visas. *The Economic and Labour Relations Review*, 24(3), 340–361.

Vertovec, S. (2006). Is circular migration the way forward in global policy?. *Around the Globe*, 3(2), 38–44.

Wellard, S. J. and Stockhausen, L. J. (2010). Overseas trained nurses working in regional and rural practice settings: Do we understand the issues? *Rural and Remote Health*, 10, 1458 (online). www.rrh.org.au. Accessed 28.11.11.

Wendt, J. (2010). *Nice Work*. Melbourne: Melbourne University Publishing.

Winkelmann-Gleed, A. (2006). *Migrant Nurses: Motivation, Integration and Contribution*. Radcliffe Publishing, World Health Organisation. www.who.int/workforcealliance/brain-drain_brain-gain/en/

Workplace Gender Equality Agency (WGEA). (2015). *Gender Composition of the Workforce: By Industry*. www.wgea.gov.au. Accessed 6.1.19.

World Health Organization. The WHO Global Code of Practice on the International Recruitment of Health Personnel. Geneva: WHO: 2010. http://www.who.int/hrh/migration/code/practice/en/.

World Health Organisation (WHO). (2018). www.who.int/hrh/events/2018/women-in-health-workforce/en/. Accessed 5.5.19.

Wright, C. F., Groutsis, D., and van den Broek, D. (2017). Employer-sponsored temporary labour migration schemes in Australia, Canada and Sweden: Enhancing efficiency, compromising fairness? *Journal of Ethnic and Migration Studies*, 43(11), 1854–1872.

Xu, Y. (2007). Strangers in strange lands: A metasynthesis of lived experiences of immigrant Asian nurses working in Western countries. *Advances in Nursing Science*, 30(3), 246–265.

Yeates, N. (2004). Global care chains. *International Feminist Journal of Politics*, 6(3), 369–391.

Yeates, N. (2009). Production for export: The role of the state in the development and operation of global care chains. *Population, Space and Place*, 15(2), 175–187.

Young, S. and Madden, R. (1992). *Immigration Selection Policies Affecting Women and Men*. In Proceedings of Second National Immigration Outlook Conference. Pp. 252–259.

3 From Incheon in Korea to Bankstown

Jo's Story

Introduction

When you first meet Jo, you are immediately swept into the relentless movement of her body. Jo talks the way she works and thinks, quickly, as she reflects on her past: her eyes darting with intensity. Listening to Jo's life story it would be easy to conclude that she earned her position as the Nurse Unit Manager at a large outer-metropolitan Sydney public hospital through sheer work and determination. But as you become drawn into Jo's spirit and her energy, you also realise how contagious her life force is. Although tiny in stature, Jo draws people in through her perpetual humour, optimism, continual laugh, and her lively communication. Her energy and enthusiasm command the respect of both her patients and her junior and senior colleagues.

Working as a Nurse Unit Manager at Bankstown Hospital seems a perfect job for a dynamo like Jo. Located around 20 kilometres south-west of Sydney, Bankstown is a vibrant and diverse area with comparatively high surrounding unemployment. It is home to an emerging migrant community with a particularly large Muslim representation. According to the Australian Bureau of Statistics, almost 60% of this suburb speaks a language other than English at home (compared to less than 40% of the broader Sydney population). Outside English, the dominant language spoken in Bankstown homes is Arabic (21% compared to 4% in greater Sydney). There are also five times more Bankstown residents that speak Vietnamese; twice as many residents who speak Greek; and four times more residents who speak Macedonian at home. The multicultural mix of the community base in this region is clear as are the complexities of patient care.

Like a lot of recently settled migrants who reside and/or work in Bankstown, the here and now for Jo is the result of many significant twists and turns. While she has been in Australia for several decades now, Jo was born in January 1958 in Chungcheongnam-do province, South Korea. This province is known for its transportation connections by rail and road between Seoul and other major cities in the southern region of South Korea.

Jo describes Korea during her early life as 'just nothing'. Rather than a negative comment about how she feels about her homeland, it is a reflection of the time, during and shortly after the Korean War (1950–1953). 'Just nothing' means that many Koreans in the South were able to do little else other than survive. Life during these years was reduced to a series of post-war infrastructure and community rebuilding activities. At this time, even registering the birth of a new child was considered by many to be unnecessary or extravagant. Only the wealthy and the status-conscious registered births. Therefore, Jo's parents did not register her birth until she was one year old because, according to Jo, 'surviving was more important'. When Jo recounts this anecdote, you get a sense of her attitude to work and life. It is almost as if her birth story encapsulates the decisions she subsequently makes about where she travels and what she does with her life: the die had been cast. The direction that Jo takes, and her pragmatism in action, seems to unfold in an irreversible and unstoppable manner.

As a young child, around the age of six or seven, Jo and her family, which included her parents and her two brothers and sister, drove 100 kilometres north, to a town called Incheon, which forms an outer rim to the sprawling city of Seoul. This move proved to be the first of many stepping-stones in Jo's life and career. When she decided to pursue a nursing career at the age of 19, Seoul was within striking distance of Saudi Arabia to which she travelled; and from there to Australia.

Being 'there'

The arrival of over 75,000 Soviet-backed North Korean People's Army sol-diers into the southern pro-Western Republic of Korea sparked the Korean War in 1950. In July 1950, American troops entered South Korea to fight and quash what it saw as the escalation of international communism. During the three-year duration of the Korean war, some five million soldiers and civilians lost their lives. Looking back, one could be forgiven for think-ing that the fight waged against communism by the US was given greater priority than the protection of human life. Indeed in 1950, a National Secu-rity Council report recommended that the US would do whatever it took to contain communist expansionism, regardless of the implications. This was, after all the Cold War where powerful interests were being played out.

As a result of that war, the separation of North and South Korea remains to this day, as does a two-mile-wide demilitarised zone separating Korea. When Jo describes herself as a 'baby boomer', she is referencing the Korean War, rather than the Second World War. Born just five years after overt hos-tilities ceased, Jo grew up in a country that was rebuilding and reinventing itself under the influence and watchful eye of allies including the US.

She was also growing up in a deeply traditional culture undergoing strik-ing transition. During and after the Korean War, where the main priority for Jo and her family was survival, community was everything, particularly in this post-war period when people were trying to rebuild their lives to resem-ble life as it had been before the war. Jo describes her father as having a particularly important place within the community as an '*Eejung*'. The term describes someone who knows the town intimately, including how many people live in the community, what jobs people have, and 'everything that happens in the town of Incheon'. He collected the census information for the government and in doing so, gained respect as a community leader. He assisted in the building of the local primary school and Jo's house was often used to billet newly arrived schoolteachers until they found a place to live. In addition to this core community role, the family made a living from being entrepreneurs acting as 'middlemen', travelling between farms collecting grains and other primary products, to distribute for sale at the local market.

The Confucian tradition of respecting others and living ethically by adopting a good attitude and strong social etiquette was as important to Jo's family as it was to the wider Korean society. Respecting one's parents and the elderly remains a guiding principle for Jo today.

When she was young, this principle was reflected in both a diligent obedi-ence of her parents' wishes but a quiet independence of spirit. Her mother would always say that her first daughter was a very well-disciplined child, much more disciplined than her brothers and sister. She did what her mother asked, but also showed independence and self-determination from an early age. She recalls that every night when she was two or three years-old, she would carefully fold her clothes and place them beside her bed. Her mother would remark that she was very good at looking after herself. It transpires that she is very good at looking after others also. On reflection she said:

> *In Korean the saying is that you're born with your personality. You can't change it. But then of course it'll change a little bit by external forces and circumstances. But actually God gives you your personality. That's the best way. If mum says you go to school, you go to school. After school study, homework then play. That's just a normal part of life.*

It didn't seem like Jo's mother needed to convince her to work hard at school because education was always a priority for her. From an early age she knew she wanted to do something with her life. At the time she thought of becoming either a lawyer or a teacher because in Korea the legal profession had prestige and the teaching profession had respect. Her father heavily influenced this emphasis on education and like many Korean parents, believed that education was by far the best gift that you could give your children. That belief has always stuck with Jo. Like her parents, Jo thought that an education offered you the chance to change your life for the better.

The leadership qualities that would be developed as she progressed through her nursing career emerged during her early school years. Jo, like her brother, became an 'A' student. She took school very seriously. Because she was 'always good at following orders', she was selected to be a class prefect, sharpening her leadership skills through her formative years.

While she worked very hard, her ambition to become a lawyer was more difficult to attain than she thought. Jo didn't get the required academic results to study law and, with her brother already at university, the fees were more than her parents could afford. The dream of pursuing a teaching career also became elusive, though for reasons more difficult to fathom. To be a schoolteacher in Korea, at the time, applicants not only had to have the required academic attainment but also conform to height restrictions. According to Jo, teachers in Korea had to be over 150 cm tall. Standing just shy of these height requirements, Jo's dream of being a teacher were dashed.

A scholarship to study nursing would solve the problem of her parents needing to cover the cost of her fees. Importantly for Jo, some universities also offered more comprehensive scholarship schemes that included full board. Choices for Jo included the South Korean Military Hospital and the National Medical Centre College. Along with forty other students that were accepted that year, Jo chose the Medical Centre College where she boarded on campus for three years.

The National Medical Centre College was opened in 1958. Their teaching staff was made up of European and American doctors. In the period after the Korean War, the Medical Centre, appeared modern and luxurious to Jo with the college dormitory air-conditioned and centrally-heated. Today, the choices for South Korean student nurses are much broader. Companies such as Samsung, LG and Hyundai now own Korean hospitals that surpass many Australian hospitals in their technological advancement and career development opportunities.

When reflecting on her career, Jo noted that her mother had told her that as a young girl, she would faint at the sight of blood. She had never coped well with the sight of injuries and was the first one who would be screaming and looking desperately away. Her mother asked: '*how can that kind of girl be a nurse?*'.

You get the strong sense that Jo chose nursing to ensure that she would not 'burden' her family. She did not want to, and has never depended on her parents financially and taking a nursing scholarship was the perfect way to guarantee her independence. Indeed, as it transpired, Jo became the primary breadwinner for her family soon after she qualified.

Nursing was also a good way to fulfil another long-held desire—to travel.

> *Since I was young, I just always wanted to go America because at that time America was a big thing in our country. After the Korean War America gave us food. So, a lot of Korean people, poor people got food from them. So, I have always had a good image of America as a rich country. So, I was dying to go there.*

The unique opportunities that a nursing career can provide are well documented. 'Your cap is your passport', a well-known recruiting slogan used during the 1960s to encourage Filipino nurses to the US, encapsulates these opportunities and Jo's desire for travel through work reflects this. America however, was not such an easy country to travel to at that time and Jo had to remain in Seoul for three years working as a nurse at the National Medical Centre as a condition of her college scholarship.

Soon after qualifying as a nurse, the Korean Government implemented a strategy, common throughout many Asian countries, of growing the economy through remittances. As part of a broader government labour placement strategy to 'grow the country', Korean men went to work in the mines in Germany, while the women went to Saudi Arabia to work as nurses. After completing her second compulsory year at the hospital in 1983, around 60 nurses, including Jo, applied for and secured positions working in hospitals in Saudi Arabia. This was the first time that Jo had travelled outside her home country and made 'big' money.

Being ' in-between'

Working in Saudi Arabia was, and remains, a well-known path for many nurses, particularly those from non-English-speaking countries where wages and working conditions are by comparison relatively low. Many of Jo's senior colleagues in Seoul had applied to work in Saudi Arabia and had talked of the high, tax-free wages that could be sent to family back home.

The overseas placements in countries like Saudi Arabia were highly controlled and coordinated by the Korean Government. Once there, all of the international nurses including Jo were provided with transportation to and from their gated living quarters to the hospital where they worked. These secure, gated communities came replete with Korean cooks and cleaners, so that workers were only expected to clean their individual room and their own uniforms. Working long hours and a six-day week and provided with one free trip home each year, these nurses managed to earn almost double what they had earned in Korea.

Such arrangements have become commonplace more recently. Today in Bahrain, Kuwait, Oman, Qatar, Saudi Arabia and the United Arab Emirates, 75% of physicians and 79% of nurses are non-nationals of the country, residing temporarily for work purposes in the respective countries. Similar to conditions today, back in the 1980s Jo worked alongside nurses from the UK, Pakistan, India, Egypt, China, Korea and the Philippines, among others, and enjoyed the camaraderie that often comes with people who are foreigners living and working in a new and unfamiliar country.

As is the case of the strict cultural mores determining what is acceptable and what is not for expatriates to do in Saudi Arabia, Jo and her nurse colleagues also had to adhere to strict social conventions that included not meeting with men while they were working in Saudi Arabia, and not drinking alcohol in public. Jo recalled that such activities were seen as incredibly risky. While a sense of surveillance was omnipresent, it was difficult to identify when it wasn't happening as police often did not wear uniforms and citizens could also inform police when others behaved unacceptably. Jo spoke of nurses being deported back to their home countries when caught with men or drinking. Even a suspicion of sexual interaction could result in the nurse being escorted to the maternity hospital where she would be instructed to undertake a vaginal swab to prove that no intercourse had taken place.

As Jo notes, these laws were enforced to the letter and punishments could be severe. Unlike many other countries in the world, here, guest worker behaviour outside working hours directly impacted on employment arrangements. So, if you are a woman suspected of drinking in public or meeting with men, you not only risk arrest, but are also likely to face immediate termination of your employment contract, including the loss of any benefits that you may have accrued.

For Jo personally these rules were insignificant. Not only did she not have or desire a boyfriend at the time, but she also didn't drink or smoke and had no interest in these pastimes while working in Saudi Arabia. As with many nurses there, her focus was to work hard and earn money to send home to support her family. These remittances became crucial as the family business began to fail and Jo's father's health swiftly deteriorated following a severe stroke. When he passed away, Jo became the main breadwinner for the family.

Jo's responsibility as family breadwinner was because no one could provide in the same way that she could. Her sister and brother had married and now had their own families to provide for, and her eldest brother was busy studying chemical engineering at university. To help her family, throughout her four-year contract between 1983 and 1987 in Saudi Arabia, Jo sent all of her earnings back to her mother, supporting the family's expenses and her brother's education.

It was during this period in Saudi Arabia that Jo met other nurses planning to migrate to Australia. At the time Jo knew nothing about Australia except for the rather unfortunate historic fact that it had enforced a Whites-only immigration policy. She remembered as a child that she thought it impossible for an Asian to migrate to Australia and so, she had put this dream firmly out of her mind. However, over time she came to learn that the White Australia Policy had been abolished in the late 1960s. At this point Australia became a viable possibility.

Recognising that she would need to improve her English language skills, Jo enrolled to study English in Melbourne in 1987. The transition process was rather more complicated and arduous than she had experienced in Saudi Arabia. There was no gated community, no bus to pick her up to take her to work, no cook or cleaner and, most importantly, no job. Jo's day-to-day existence would be more difficult than anything she had experienced in the past. Having worked in highly professional nursing environments in both Korea and Saudi Arabia Jo had accrued years of experience while also refining and developing her nursing skills. Yet, upon arriving in Australia Jo had to start from scratch both professionally and personally: finding a way to maintain her professional identity after transitioning into a new health care system on the other side of the world would prove to be very challenging.

The waitressing job Jo took when she initially arrived in Melbourne, and the temporary shared house where she was staying, was a long way from the supportive and secure professional and home life she had led in Korea and in Saudi Arabia. Personally, and professionally she felt like she was going backwards. After several months of enduring challenging circumstances, she took her chances and decided to move north to Sydney. The night train from Melbourne delivered her to a new city where she dispatched letters of interest with her CV to various hospitals in an attempt to secure the nursing work she was trained for and was experienced in. The best offer she received was as an assistant nurse at a nursing home based in the eastern Sydney suburb of Randwick.

There is an obvious sense of pain and sadness etched on Jo's face and in her voice when she recounts this period of her life: her tears are a physical manifestation of the loneliness, fear, sense of worthlessness and isolation. The daily struggles are still real to her when she recalls them—even after some three decades. Jo remembers the night shifts she secured at the nursing home and the commute to and from work being arduous and at times scary and daunting. She reflected: *"I was a single Asian woman. I was very slim. Walking at night it's not safe. Maybe safer than now. But still not safe. Also getting a taxi was expensive. I was saving money I have to walk home in the evening. So I used to walk a lot of the way."* This was a hard slog on top of her long shifts. Life had taken a different turn for Jo.

The job itself was both more physically demanding and filled with largely routine and menial tasks. Nurses working in Korean hospitals were never required to clean the wards or lift patients between beds and wheelchairs. Four years in a state-of-the-art Saudi hospital had not equipped her for the tasks she was now expected to perform. Jo was doing seven- or eight-hour shifts showering, changing patients' soiled nappies, serving the food and mopping floors rather than undertaking clinical nursing procedures such as performing tests. Her memories of this period are of physical exhaustion, disappointment and loneliness.

Despite the low pay and poor working conditions, Jo had a strong fatalism about what was 'meant to be'. Her displeasure at the sight of blood as a young girl paradoxically reinforced her belief that this profession was her 'calling'. She remained working at the nursing home while sending out countless application letters to Sydney Metropolitan and rural hospitals in NSW.

Three and a half months after she arrived in Sydney, Jo secured a nursing job at Liverpool hospital where she found herself in the company of nurses from many different nations including Indonesia, the Philippines, Germany, Czechoslovakia, South America, South Africa and Hong Kong to name a few. At the same time, she commenced the three-month registration process that would allow her to gain skills accreditation and registration and once again reclaim her status and work as a registered nurse.

Being 'here'

In many ways Jo is now 'here'. Her migration from Korea to Saudi Arabia and then to Australia started many years ago but the process never ends. Migrants often say that they feel a sense of bifurcated belonging. The sense of belonging elsewhere and that you belong to two vastly different cultures never leaves. You never fully feel as if you wholly belong to one place but rather live somewhere between the two. These split identities are almost abstract sentiments that reflect how daily life might be lived in one place while never really departing completely from the other. Many migrants remain engaged in the affairs of both their families and communities in their home countries while also building new families and friendships in their new country.

As a small girl America was the destination of Jo's dreams. But her new reality in Australia meant that Jo felt that she has made some real progress both professionally and personally. Australia did not end up being the stepping-stone to America but was the country she would stay in and build her own family. These decisions are often not planned out in detail. Lives unfold in the most unexpected ways for all of us, migrants in particular. However, what is clear is that Jo now finds herself in a working and living situation that reflects her level of expertise and which gave her the stability and confidence that she sought after arriving in Australia. Her nursing identity was now more secure and this security allowed her the opportunity to give back to others what she had learnt over her twenty-five-year career.

'Being here' however did come with many challenges. Like many other nurses who have come from non-English-speaking backgrounds, Jo felt that *"because you don't speak English perfectly you've got to show something to 'match up' with locally trained nurses. You have to work so much harder than anybody else"*. There are always sensitivities around how different cultures communicate and Jo's fierce work ethic and fast-talking endears her to many of her colleagues while also driving many of her professional accomplishments. This is also reflected in her dedication to forming patient relationships. However, discrimination from colleagues and patients has also been an unfortunate reality. According to Jo there are two kinds of patients:

> *One type of patient—are beautiful, so lovely and they try to take you in and understand who you are. Where you originally come from, they don't really care and they're all lovely. But unfortunately, there are another group of patients who think that she is 'just Asian'.*

All too often Jo has been asked when she had come out on the boat. The assumption that she is a Vietnamese refugee gives you a flavour of the stigmatising and stereotyping of migrants from an Asian background, a lumping together of an ethnically and culturally diverse group, which is not uncommon in Australia. Even though she might try to explain to patients that she arrived in Australia by plane with a very different cultural heritage, she often gets the sense that she is not seen as equal in the eyes of some.

Over the years Jo has learnt to deal patiently but sternly when such situations arise, reprimanding patients when they make racist remarks to her. In her role as Nursing Unit Manager Jo is in a powerful position and able to rebuke negative attitudes. She actively intervenes when newly arrived migrant nurses suffer the brunt of racist sentiments.

The existence of a 'global care chain' means that countries like Australia have become dependent on migrant health professionals throughout the post-World War II period. Indeed, Australia is one of the few high-income countries that have specific migration policies to encourage health professionals to come here for work purposes. Therefore, you would not expect that patients in hospital wards to yell, *"Go back to your own country"* at nurses.

Go to any ward in any Australian hospital and you will immediately identify the diversity of health personnel. However, for some patients it seems that old habits are hard to change. The hospital ward may be the first time that a patient may have come into close contact with someone from a non-English-speaking background. As such, these interchanges between patient and nurse may represent the front line of where negative race relations play out. It is a situation that is intensified given the need for patients to trust and respect the nurses that care for them over a period of several days and possibly weeks.

Jo realised a long time ago that it was important to stand up for herself in her relationships and to educate both her colleagues and her patients about the value of difference and the need to respect acknowledge and make room for the inclusion of 'difference'. As we visit Jo's workplace at Bankstown Hospital the pressure of her daily activities is obvious. The front-line managers, including Jo as a Nurse Unit Manager, are expected to balance the day-to-day running of the unit including work allocation, patient relations and human resource issues, payroll and staffing within an extremely stretched health system. While the managers might have the training to undertake these tasks, they have little time to manage any potential conflicts that relate to diversity, inclusion, equality and respect. Despite the need to have collegial relations for the smooth running of the ward and the health system more broadly, the stretched system makes these developmental and important activities difficult to incorporate into daily work.

While Jo reflects on the pressures of her work, she says that she now feels 'lucky' that she has pursued a nursing career. As a younger woman she rarely thought about whether she liked nursing or not. She 'just worked'. With nursing she knew she would develop a career and learn, she knew she could travel, and she knew she could also look after her family in Korea financially. Despite her initial desire to teach or practise law, nursing developed more fatalistically. Like many (particularly older) nurses will tell you, nursing is often seen as a type of calling. As Jo recounted, *"There must be a reason for it, not academic. . . . I never thought to be a nurse. But since I have become a nurse, I have never regretted it. I love it. I loved it. I love my job. I love my patients, they're family. I just love them."*

Jo married an Australian in 1988 and in 1990 she returned to university to undertake postgraduate studies in nursing. The pressures of her job, being married and eventually having two children has not slowed her down or dimmed her interest in further study. *"I'd be doing it anyhow. I wanted a PhD, but too late, and I haven't got time!"*

Over the years Jo has become more embedded into Australian life, both professionally and personally. After the birth of her children she has resettled her mother in Australia. Her mother is less integrated into Australian society, but she has joined an elderly group and a church group that keep her connected to and involved with the Korean community.

While Jo has become more accustomed to the Australian way of life and nursing practice, she has not forgotten how she felt when she first arrived. She has built strong links with the Korean nursing community to help newly migrant nurses overcome the personal and professional challenges of building a life in Australia, becoming a central and leading member of the Korean Nurses Association. The numerous, seemingly insignificant challenges can easily become big challenges when there is no one available to help with the transition process to a new country. There may be no one available to explain the many small social and cultural idiosyncrasies, differences in professional registration and accreditation processes, and differences in nursing practices such as the lines of authority and modes of communication that are different from one culture and nursing system to another.

> *You have to work hard, because number one, you are not familiar with the Australian culture and system and the language. Australian English is different from American, and especially for me at the time. The Pommy English and Irish English and Scottish. I couldn't understand [any] English. I know now, I can tell.*

After working at Bankstown hospital as the Nurse Unit Manager, Jo was invited to give a presentation for the Korean Nurses Association, which was set up in 1998. After her presentation that day she realised that the Association needed to be strengthened and reinvigorated. She felt a need to develop and build on her Korean roots by supporting services which would help newly arrived migrant nurses feel a greater sense of belonging and assist with their pathway into the workplace. She quickly became the President of the Association that now has nearly 50 members and collaborates through the process of monthly meetings and professional development workshops.

There is a strong sense that now that she is well established it is important to give back in some way. In this case she is giving back to both countries, the Korean nurses that follow the same path as she did, and the Australian health system that relies on the professionalism of their nursing staff.

> *That's what I teach them, because I never got any support from anywhere. It took me so long, years, to be an educator. It took so long to become a manager. But now, if I have a junior here, I talk with them. I have a simple interview with them about the job, about the need for study. I can give them all the advice. There are options there, I can advise. I can do that easily for anybody.*

'Being here' means that Jo is now an Australian citizen. As she says: *"a good citizen. A role-model citizen. But at the same time, I won't forget my heritage. It's Korean. So, I want all my Korean Australians to do the right thing"*.

4   Meifang

Steering the Inner Drive

Introduction

Meifang, or Mei as she prefers to be called mentions in passing that she had been married for seven or eight years. She had met her husband one night ballroom dancing after work with friends. She was 24 and her husband-to-be was a 36-year-old navy officer. They married in 2000 and the photos that Mei produces on our second meeting over a traditional tea in her home, show a couple happy on their wedding day. However, throughout her years of work and travel in Australia and other countries, Mei's husband has remained in China. Although still married, she reflects now: *"Probably because I was so focused on work, I neglected my marriage"*.

As we listen to her story it is clear that Mei is very work-focused, very driven, privileging professional advancements over personal happiness and deeper connections. Her career has taken her to many countries and to her most recent decision to move from nursing to commence a degree in dentistry, but it was nursing that triggered her desire to move abroad, to travel and search for harmony.

Being 'there'

Mei was born in 1976 and grew up in the rural rice fields of Hunchun (meaning Borderland), a small town located in an Eastern Province of China, bordering North Korea and Russia. The year 1976 was prescient and momentous. In April, Zhou Enlai, who was the first Premier of the People's Republic of China, serving from 1949, died. Later that year, Mao Zedong died. Significant democracy demonstrations were also violently suppressed during this year and by October, the Cultural Revolution had ended and the Gang of Four were arrested. In July of that year the Tangshan earthquake also killed over 250,00 people. Both man-made and natural turmoil marked the year of Mei's birth.

However, Mei's family were far removed from these tumultuous events, living 40 minutes' drive from Hangzhou and two hours' drive south of Shanghai. Mei's village life was simple, humble and frugal. Like many other Chinese families, Mei's mother focused on raising her children (Mei and her brother, who was born four years earlier).

The One Child Policy, introduced just three years after Mei was born in 1979, was implemented to reduce social, economic and environmental problems and if couples violated the one-child policy they faced the possibility of financial penalties, loss of employment or, on occasion, forced abortions. Mei's family were lucky to have avoided this policy by a matter of only a few years.

Mei led a simple rural life. In the early 1980s there were few of the benefits of Chinese economic development and global ties that we see today. Her family managed by selling noodles; rice; chickens; pigs and ducks at the local markets. While they subsisted as small farmers, her eyes lit up as she described the colourful world she occupied at this time in her life, which was also full of responsibilities. As a young girl Mei helped the family by taking on household chores particularly during harvest season: *"cleaning the house and cooking the family meals"*. When she wasn't helping her parents, Mei spent her time playing in rice fields, fishing and reading comic books or novels or listening to the radio. Reminiscing, Mei said her favourite job during school holidays was to look after the family ducks, taking them out into the fields in the morning and ushering them back in the evening.

While seemingly idyllic, Mei has a sense of unease about her upbringing and her family. She reflects now: *"there's not much harmony. Even now when I am back home, when I would go out with my parents, and with my brother, I don't feel that inner peace and harmony"*.

The inner peace and harmony Mei talks about is hard to identify exactly, however expectations shaped by her gender may have played a role. She recalls that her brother was always at the 'centre' of the family's attention. In China during the 1970s a young girl's role in the family ran a very conventional path. There were expectations as a result of being a woman. You were expected to secure a stable income; marry, settle down and support your family. While she visibly defies her 37 years, she notes that even now, her parents remind her of these expectations each time she returns to visit them.

When she was 14, Mei had the opportunity to attend nursing training college in Hangzhou, the capital of Zhejiang Province. Mei certainly had the academic capacity and curiosity to complete a nursing degree, having topped most of her classes during her school years. While not knowing exactly what nursing involved, this move met the approval of her parents and legitimised their community standing. Despite her tender age, Mei felt a sense of freedom for the first time to escape the routine village and dull family life. My heart was filled with excitement and hope.

Given the small allowance the Chinese Government provided for students and with some pocket money from her parents, she was proud to be semi-independent from her family at last. Incentivising such training was part of a larger plan for the Chinese Government which trained nurses for export by negotiating international labour supply agreements with Saudi Arabia and the US. For example, in 2002/3 a training centre was established in Beijing for nurses to gain accreditation and certification for their nursing education, qualifications and English proficiency to secure work in the US, leading to a strategy known as 'brain power stored overseas'. Mei knew that she would have to move to larger urban centres to develop confidence and capability to move overseas; a prospect that was envisaged with optimism and excitement. Soon after she graduated, Mei took the first step to an international nursing career.

Being 'there' in a Nursing Career

At 17, Mei was relatively young when she graduated from nursing school. Perhaps this, and her rural background, explains why she felt—what she described as being—culturally and intellectually inferior among 'city people'. Determined to overcome her feelings of inferiority she embarked on forays into journalism, writing for the local newspaper and the hospital monthly journal, going on to study English and Chinese literature. Mei had few friends in the city who shared her interests so study became very 'innate' for Mei and filled the loneliness while feeding her soul.

In spite of the over-supply of nurses in China at the time, Mei found a position relatively quickly. Then after nine years working in a traditional Chinese hospital, she earned herself a much-coveted position in a foreign-managed hospital affiliated with Zhejiang University. This hospital was unique because it was the first in China to receive international accreditation signifying high clinical standards and exemplary safety and patient care. It also received an AAA-rating which exceeds the highest national standards set by the Ministry of Health. The Hong Kong philanthropist and movie mogul, Sir Run Run Shaw, donated the hospital as part of a HK$6.5 billion donation to charities, schools and hospitals in Hong Kong and mainland China (Connell, 2010).[1]

The hospital also had strong links to the US through the Loma Linda Medical Centre in California and Mei absorbed both the clinical and religious experiences this position offered. A Seventh-day Adventist facility, the Loma Linda Hospital was famous for its infant heart transplants. Mei's experience at the hospital not only broadened her professional training but it also put her in contact with many health professionals who had that faith. Upon her return in 2007 from exchange to California, she started a Master's degree at Zhejiang University. Her supervisor was a neuroscientist who had just returned from Belgium and his devotion to Christianity fed her interest in religion and again ignited her soul-searching and inner drive.

Exposure to an international environment raised Mei's awareness of the importance of English language skills in accessing future career opportunities. While inspired to work overseas, there was one unlikely opportunity that emerged. In November 2002 the first case of the deadly SARS virus erupted in China. While many staff refused to treat SARS patients, Mei was one of the few volunteers given the documented health risks. Mei recounts:

I didn't worry. I just felt excited that I could do something. There were four SARS patients in our city. They were all moved into an infectious zone. One level of the hospital was set up as their ward. All the doctors and other health professionals who had been recruited into this hospital, including psychiatrists, looked after those patients. We also lived in the hospital. We couldn't go out because we were a risk. We were carriers because we were in touch with the patients. So, we lived there.

We wore three layers of masks and bodysuits which were very hot and uncomfortable. One of our four patients died. They were all Chinese. It was very scary because a lot of nurses and doctors in other hospitals died when they caught the infection.

Her experiences caring for SARS patients during the epidemic led to promotions and her 'old English uniform with a little paper hat' was worn as a symbol of pride for Mei. By 2001, China had joined the World Trade Organisation and was well on the road to becoming one of the world's most formidable economies. Chinese citizens were now allowed to own property, rent apartments and move freely between provinces to find work. The world around her was changing quickly but Mei was searching for something more.

It was during this period that Mei met her husband at a ballroom dancing event. She reflected, chuckling, as she recounted the story:

> *He isn't a very good dancer and he's not really interested in dancing, but he went there with his friends because it was a good place to meet a girl. We went out together a few times and then we began to get close. My parents didn't like him very much, but they never agreed with anything I did. He was born and grew up in Shanghai. After his father retired, their family moved to Hangzhou where they lived in a really beautiful area. Then his father wanted him to join the Navy or Army, so he joined the Navy and travelled around China. Finally, he returned to Hangzhou where he met me.*

While separated for many years, the bond between Mei and her husband is clear, speaking tenderly about their shared vision and the freedom his support has afforded her:

> *I think he has a vision that we can have a future much bigger than we have in China. He has even taken the risk that he could lose me. He loves me and he has always believed in me. Even when we separated, I returned to visit him, and he has also visited here. He's still very loyal to me. He visits my parents very often, as I would do if I was in China. So, this is really gracious of him.*

While Mei's job at the international hospital offered more interesting work opportunities than were available through other hospitals, many of her nursing friends had joined the government-sponsored labour initiatives and migrated for work to Saudi Arabia. While Mei found this prospect exciting, the restrictions placed on nurses living in Saudi Arabia were not. She looked elsewhere and remembered an old school friend who had migrated to Melbourne to work as a nurse. This was the path that Mei decided to follow.

Rather than take the easy route to stay with friends in Melbourne, Mei decided to head to Perth. Passing the International English language (IELTS) test was tough and success rates are notoriously very low. For example, even for Chinese nurses whose secondary schooling was in English, the pass rate has been reported to be as low as 20%.[2] Overcoming her first hurdle, Mei was accepted on a student visa to undertake a one-year bridging course. While ready for a new beginning, this turning point in Mei's life was marked by a strange tension between leaving and staying. She recounted that in China her work was challenging and involved managing a large team in a hospital and life was kind of happy in a lot of ways. *"But I still could not resist the temptation I can go outside and have something new. So, I came."*

Being 'in-between'

Once on the plane, Mei's heart was filled with excitement, fearlessness and anticipation about what lay ahead. She had little idea about her future or the country she was about to arrive in. Landing in Perth at 10.30 pm, Mei remembers that it felt like an uninhabited isolated wilderness. Indeed, as the capital city of Australia's largest state, with a population of about 1.9 million people, it is described as one of the most isolated capital cities in the world. In fact, the city is closer to Denpasar Indonesia, than to other Australian centres such as Brisbane, Sydney and Melbourne, all of which are approximately 4,000 kilometres away on the east coast.

Mei knew this was going to be a transitional year and she prepared herself for the uncertainty, loneliness, isolation, frustration and struggle. Her first pressure test emerged when she discovered that the AUD $3,000 10-week bridging course she had enrolled in had a very low graduation rate, where, of the 30 or so students who completed it, only around five or six students had passed. Mei's fears were allayed as she passed, noting that *"failing was totally unacceptable for me"*. Buoyed by this success, she secured a part-time job at a homecare facility in Perth and purchased a car.

As was to happen many times later, this job in home care was sourced through church networks. Mei had a consistent strategy of using the church to integrate into the new community. Disappointingly, she found that this first job was definitely a significant downgrade from her previous position at the hospital at the Zhejiang University. The home-care position required no management skills or advanced clinical knowledge. Instead, she worked as a nurse's assistant. But Mei was appreciative of the work because it helped her gain insights into the local aged care sector and it allowed her to practise her English language skills in a low risk environment.

Mei noted the different cultural and institutional nuances that she observed in her first workplace experience. Compared to Australia, the home- and aged-care sector is under-developed in China. While China also has an aging population, health and long-term care for the aged is largely a family matter. As such, the aged-care sector has far less coverage and good-quality, structured training for staff working in the sector is minimal. Also, unlike Australia, where private, or government entities dominate the sector, in China the sector is almost entirely government-run.[3] As well as these observable workplace differences, there were also other hurdles to overcome in order to practise nursing in Australia. The road to registration required Mei to undertake further education, complete a raft of paperwork and navigate her way through the bureaucratic maze while dealing with the financial strain. In order to apply for the conversion course and to prepare for nurse registration in Australia, Mei needed an additional $20,000 to pay the fees.

Developing Professional Identity

Since graduating from nursing school at the age of 17, Mei had been self-sufficient financially. At the time she decided to come to Australia, she had already had 15 years' working experience. Post-marriage, Mei's husband also supported her financially and emotionally—particularly with regards to her educational pursuits. She reflects that:

> *When I came to Australia, he gave me our family savings. He believed that he should support me, and he liked to support me. He encouraged me to do what I really want to do.*

In 2010, just as Mei passed the English exam, she also gained her registration and quickly sent it to hundreds of potential employers. She swiftly heard back from three hospitals with an offer of employment. Wrongly assuming that urban and rural hospitals would be equally well resourced, and also assuming that a public hospital might offer better training opportunities than a private one, Mei accepted the Wagga Wagga public hospital offer and boarded her flight to Wagga Wagga via Sydney.

Situated about 450 kilometres south-west of Sydney, Wagga Wagga (meaning 'the place of many crows' in Wiradjuri) is the largest inland town in NSW, supporting a population of around 60,000, with only around 6% of inhabitants born outside of Australia compared to over 28% for Australia nationally. When Mei arrived in Wagga Wagga her, *"heart was totally thrown into a deeper sea. This is like a desert in the middle of nowhere"*. Unable to wrestle any positivity, Mei felt that the hospital was very 'backward' and the buildings were poorly restored and patient facilities outdated. While accustomed to working with electrical beds in China, now she had to contend with heavy manual beds that were unforgiving on a nurse's back. The abounding country kindness did not overcome her disappointment about the hospital conditions. Fortuitously, the bureaucracy that Mei faced to secure her employment provided an opportunity for her to reconsider the Wagga position. While waiting for her final paperwork she flew to Sydney to investigate her second option, the North Shore Private Hospital. She visited the hospital and immediately moved to Sydney.

The new position also switched Mei to a new clinical area of orthopaedics. Shifting between specialties and wards allowed for new opportunities, but there were also frustrations. Mei applied for Clinical Nursing Specialist positions in which she had considerable experience but was overlooked. She put this down to being an 'overseas-' trained nurse, feeling that the hospital preferred local nurses more familiar with the Australian system. As usual, Mei overcame potential barriers to advancement by embarking on further education.

While professionally things were falling into place, socialising outside work proved difficult. Although happy to participate in out-of-work activities, Mei rarely felt fully engaged in the social activities. While comfortable in her social group, the mix of personal and professional was quite different from her experiences of Chinese work culture. For example, the Australian tradition of 'just simply going out for a good time' was new to her.

> *When I first started attending lots of social outings for example, the Christmas party last year or the year before was really good. Lots of drinking, dancing and having a good time. But for me (in China) these events were something where you look back on the year, what we achieved and what we're going to achieve this session. There was none of that. People simply go out drinking and have a good time. So, I feel something is missing. So, I have an identity that is split.*

The clash of identity was also fuelled by her confidence levels in her English language ability—unable to speak up as she would in China, a source of frustration which impacted on her self-esteem.

> *You know, in Chinese I can say things nicely, be firm, and be assertive. But I need to learn in an English setting how I can do this. So you know, these little things are important. I watch. I listen. I practise. But still, I'm not very good. The work culture is not very good, but I don't know how to change it. Similar things happen in China as well, but in China I was in a position to change the culture because if I am a nurse unit manager I can kind of promote the positive thinking and bring in good things. But here I'm low down and have little power to change things.*

Being 'here' (Personally) and Being 'in-between here and there'

Being Chinese and living in a Western country, Mei often feels caught in the middle of two identities—the Eastern and the Western identity. When she lived in China, she realised there was little room for religious faith. While many villagers might follow Buddhist thinking, the government opposed Buddhist ideology. Similarly, Christianity is not tolerated in China. While Mei noted that she tried to find out the meaning of life, by reading Buddhist and other spiritual books, attending lectures and seminars on faiths of various kinds, it was not until she was exposed to Christianity that she felt she found meaning. When working at the Seventh Day Adventist hospital, she met a Christian professor and joined his 'family church'. Despite government surveillance of their activities, she attended readings about the Bible. Mei continues to 'shop around for churches' because she believes that connections to any denomination of Christian church open doors that, as an outsider, may not be possible to open otherwise.

Since living in Australia Mei has attended Mandarin services, where the congregation was mainly from Taiwan or Mainland China. She found it difficult to fully engage in the culture of the church because:

> *There are certain people in charge of the group, we don't discuss it a lot. We have to follow the main opinion of the person in charge. I don't particularly like this. I like very free discussion where you have a potential to share. I tried to join in English services as well. But the English services are mainly Australian Born Chinese. I don't have that experience. I've only been here for a few years. But I like the feeling, the English service—they have this kind of free spirit that's more inclusive and more respecting your privacy and more respecting your own opinion.*

Her 'in-between status' concerns her though. She reflected that: *"I'm different because I'm a little bit Western in lots of ways, the mindset or something. For the total local Australian church, I feel it's also a little bit difficult. So, I'm juggling around. I'm still in that process"*. While she might settle on one particular denomination of church for a while she is just as likely to be shopping around churches and attending services in another one soon after.

Looking back over her career there is a sense of *"disappointment with myself and the system"*. Her high levels of training and work experience combined with her extended education have meant that Mei arrived in Australia with a very strong skill set around team management. However, she has been unable to use her skills to contribute to a collaborative work culture while in Australia. There are some strong differences between Chinese and Australian work cultures:

> *People are not really strongly related to each other in the workplace here. In China my team is like a family. So, when I was a nurse manager, I treated my team members as my family members. So every problem they can talk to me and I talk to them. We went out very regularly socially. But when a new member came in we had an introduction session, to let them introduce themselves.*

Everything is different in Australia, challenging Mei's personal and professional identity. In terms of Australian workplace culture Mei commented that: *"the connection is not really strong"* and little effort is made to integrate newcomers into work unit/s, with limited orientation activities. While her experiences of orientation have varied considerably from one hospital to another Mei feels that a more welcoming culture, more open to different ways of practising nursing and more respect to outside knowledge and skill, would help overseas-trained nurses feel their knowledge and expertise are acknowledged.

> *Nursing in Australia would eventually benefit from the skill and knowledge brought in by overseas-trained nurses. My experiences have been that the Australian nursing is based on a rather rigid mindset. It expects the newcomers to fit into their way of doing things and excludes other ways without critical thought. This is one of the reasons that lots of overseas-trained nurses feel their expertise is not important as there is only one way to go—follow the rules rather than challenge the rules for a better outcome.*

While recounting this story she pulled out the hospital newsletter she had contributed to, speaking glowingly about her interest in creating a united work culture and the importance of such workplace communication to achieve this. She shared photos of her hospital unit, her awards of recognition, a recognition that has been largely undervalued within the Australian hospital context. It is perhaps because of these occupational disconnects that Mei is embarking on a new occupational adventure by studying dentistry in Queensland. She noted that she would have stayed in nursing if there had been an open-minded working culture; more nursing specialist positions and nursing practitioner pathways to enable those with a strong inner drive to be more of a master in their own area.

From where Mei stood, it seemed that migrant nurses had to *"handle all the hardship from the senior nurses"*, both local and foreign-born. She felt that once you had accepted the fact that you were not so easily integrated, life became less difficult: *"You have to be really, really humble. You do all the shift work and you do the shifts that other people don't want"*.

Mei's professional experiences make her reflect on the restrictions surrounding her professional development and progression in Australia:

> While I've seen and done so many years of US-style management, I can see there is room for improvement in Australia, in terms of nursing management. I think there could be greater focus on organisational culture, professional development, the overall professional social image and self-image, the opportunity to make decisions and develop expertise, a more flexible hierarchy within the hospital system and more opportunities for education. But, as an outsider, it's quite difficult to change things: It is difficult to be accepted. I'm sure, there are lots of immigrant nurses who want to do better, but they need encouragement.'

The Future

Mei has studied her way through and towards many opportunities while overcoming the challenges that life has presented her with. She has studied hard and worked her way to senior positions in a prestigious hospital at Zhejiang University. Her work has taken her to America, Thailand, Singapore, Cambodia, Vietnam, Tibet and Burma but now, after six years in Australia and 20 years in the nursing profession, Mei is reviewing her life.

She searches for activities that are 'meaningful'. Since migrating to Australia, she has grown professionally and gained more freedom personally than she could have dreamt of if she had remained in China. Reflecting on her past she feels she is in a good position: *"I'm free. I can stay in Australia; I can come back to China. Maybe I have a lot of frustration and stress on the way, but my life is more interesting'*.

For Mei, the prospect of returning to China is distant. She would find it difficult *"to fit in again, because people think you should be married with children now. But you don't have this pressure in Australia"*. However, as our discussion draws to a close, Mei returns to recount her feelings of a split identity. When she returns to China, she feels:

> like a stranger and the place looks strange. This is really not the place where I grew up. Probably the people who live there are okay; they make more money, and everything seems economically better. But the environment is getting worse even though life for them is much easier than before.

However traditional vestiges continue. Mei's family feels that her absence has made her a bad daughter and each time she returns she feels there is an energy that is pushing her away:

> *I'm not the kind of personality that will be happy to stay in a secondary role. I want to be treated fairly. I don't blame my parents. They grew up in such a traditional Chinese society and they are not very educated. They are good people, but they just didn't have the opportunity to go to school and read books, so they follow all this tradition.*

While she was unsure about leaving China in 2008, she now she feels that she made the right decision:

> *My first choice is to live here. I wanted to prove to my parents that I'm equally good enough for them. But now it's not really important, because I think I'm getting mature. I know it is my life and I'm glad that I didn't surrender or settle too early and accept what I'm not really happy with. So, I'm glad.*

Mei ends our chat on a large dose of personal reflection:

> *I'm a very active person and I seek out educational opportunities. I like to learn new things. But I think now I will probably focus more on personal relationships than on chasing my goals. Because everywhere I've been, I think the most precious memories are always related to people. And I do regret that the more I have focused on my goals, the less time I have spent with people.*

Notes

1. Kingma cited in Connell 2010.
2. www.adelaidenow.com.au/news/south-australia/australian-nursing-and-midwifery-federation-says-english-test-creates-workplace-risks/story-e6frea83-1226527750168
3. Chu, L. W. and Chi, I. (2008). Nursing homes in China. *Journal of the American Medical Directors Association*, 9(4), 237–243.

Reference

Connell, J. (2010). *Migration and the Globalisation of Health Care*. Cheltenham: Edward Elgar.

5   "Don't Call Me Sister"

Cynthia's Journey From Harare to Austin and Sydney

Introduction

Often, it is the little misunderstandings and daily impressions accumulated over a period of time that can lead to a feeling of isolation. The misunderstandings between colleagues at work or between strangers from different cultures can build a sense of isolation and intensify a longing for 'home', or a desire for the familiarity of the past. These misunderstandings might result from the way a word is interpreted turning a casual conversation into an awkward exchange. As Cynthia is about to recount, expressions or colloquialisms used in one country do not seamlessly translate from one country to another. She was in stiches with laughter when she relayed this anecdote about when she first arrived in Sydney to take up a job at St Vincent's Hospital.

Three weeks after she had arrived at St Vincent's Hospital, Cynthia was participating in a team meeting. As was the custom at this hospital, the nurses working within her team at the hospital referred to each other as 'sister'. But for Cynthia, who had spent most of her life in the US, this word meant something entirely different to the way her work colleagues were using it. As she tells us:

> *So, they call each other Sister, and I'm thinking 'what the hell'? Are they trying to make me comfortable, right'? Because in the US it's more just like a black on black person like you're my sister. You know, you're like you're my girl. So, a white person's not going to be like 'yo, you're my sister'!*
>
> *So, my boss says, 'Hey Sister' and I ignore it. I'm like 'oh, (rolls her eyes) it's all good, whatever'. So, I'm thinking, he can't be racist because he's so nice to me. He's very welcoming.*
>
> *So, then the other nurse comes in, in the med room, and says 'Hey Sister'. I'm just kind of like puzzled, man. I'm like you know, I was like 'you don't have to make me feel comfortable today right'?*
>
> *Another colleague says it then I was like 'you know what, screw it'.*

A short time later at the hospital during a meeting to welcome Cynthia into the work group she felt the need to raise the point. She recounts:

> *So, they call everybody to the meeting, and I sit next to the manager. They're like 'oh welcome, Cynthia, thank you. I hope everything is great, you know'.*
>
> *I was like 'you know what, guys, I have to say something'. I'm like, 'I'm so sorry, I hope this doesn't come off as offensive but are you calling me Sister to make me feel comfortable because I don't think that's right?' My boss turned red and he's like 'No, Cynthia. St Vincent's was started by nuns and we call each other Sister, even the male nurses are Sister'.*
>
> *Everybody was like 'you're crazy' laughing. So now I'm like 'what's up, Sister'?*

As Cynthia reflected back on those first few weeks working at St Vincent's hospital in Sydney: *"maybe I was so isolated in the zone that I didn't hear it"*. There was a lot going on in Cynthia's life that would have easily distracted her. She was not only trying to integrate herself into this new workplace, but she was also worried about how well her young son might integrate into his new and sometimes strange life in Sydney.

It wasn't that 32-year-old Cynthia hadn't faced challenges before. As a teenager she had transitioned from her school in Harare to Austin, Texas, US, when she lived with her brother, who had escaped Zimbabwe many years earlier. She adapted to a new life as a single mother and then to migrating to Australia with no existing networks in Sydney. Soon after she arrived, her son, who was ten at the time, became very homesick to the point where Cynthia had little choice but to agree to have him return to live in Texas with her brother. Feeling a deep sense of loneliness and isolation with nowhere stable to live, she wondered whether she had made the right choice coming to Australia. Our opening anecdote about the misunderstanding over the use of the word 'sister' was just one of several reasons that she felt separate from her new surroundings.

Being 'there': Being Young in Zimbabwe

Cynthia was born in 1981 in a suburban area of Harare, the capital of Zimbabwe. She was the seventh, and last, child of parents who raised four boys and three girls. Her mother made a living growing cotton, working as domestic carers for local white families and her father sewed clothing and was a pastor. As a young girl, Cynthia dreamt of being a pilot but growing up in a strong Christian family, and attending church every Sunday, steered her towards a strong work ethic that involved 'helping people'.

The church was to play a guiding role throughout her life. From the family church gatherings, she attended a Baptist church and later the Covenant Church in Texas, a contemporary Christian church. Here she would find a strong ethnic mix of parishioners including Zimbabweans, Americans and Mexicans.

There were also strong role models in her own family. Her parents worked extremely hard to send her brothers to private schools in Zimbabwe in the period before independence when her mother only received minimum wages working as a maid for a white family and her father sewed clothes. Despite the humble beginnings, her brothers would say to her, *"do it, do what you can do. Push yourself!"*.

As she grew older her dream of being a pilot faded. Cynthia became more determined to get closer to a job that (in her words) *"glorified God"*. Gaining a qualification in nursing many years later therefore seemed a natural progression.

Living in Zimbabwe at that time, meant living in a country that faced major political and economic turmoil. Located just north of South Africa, the country of Zimbabwe had gained independence from the UK only one year before Cynthia was born, after it shed the white minority government of Rhodesia. After 1980 however, Robert Mugabe took control of what became an increasingly repressive and corrupt government that eliminated any opposition to his government and his supporters. Thousands of

Zimbabwean citizens were murdered and tens of thousands were tortured in military camps in the early 1980s and rigged elections made it very difficult to remove Mugabe's party from office.

Throughout this period national police prevented students and workers from staging anti-regime demonstrations as the economy stagnated. Medical staff employed in the public health sector faced deteriorating working conditions and often worked without being. These conditions continued for many years.[1] Cynthia felt that the health care system at the time was: *"not patient care. You're running a factory!"*.

There were also the various political and economic frustrations of working in the public sector of a poor country like a Zimbabwe. For instance, during the late 1990s, government workers, including nurses and doctors, often engaged in strike action over the poor wages and conditions in the sector. For a country where the national mortality rate after 1990 dropped from 60 to 42 years with nearly a quarter of the population infected by HIV, this appalling health infrastructure affected the entire Zimbabwean society and Cynthia's desire to go elsewhere.

While things may have improved over recent decades, back in the 1980s when Cynthia was a small girl, many families were desperate to help their sons leave the country to avoid being conscripted as soldiers into a war that many did not support. Many families would 'sneak' their sons out during the civil war. As brothers leave, sisters and other family members inevitably follow:

> *because usually the African tradition is the older kids take care of the younger ones. For the boys, it was to get away. My sisters ended up following for better opportunities. One brother went to England at the time. He went and he got his education and then we got our independence and he came back to Zimbabwe.*

So, Cynthia also left Zimbabwe to follow her brothers to the US to secure a future of safety and stability.

Being ' in-between': They're Like What Are You? I'm Like Well I'm From Texas but Originally Zimbabwe

Texas is a long way from Zimbabwe, both in distance and in every other way. Cynthia who was very accustomed to open space and big landscapes. In many ways Texas was a perfect place to relocate to. Given the family ties there was also never a *"thought about going anywhere else"*. The weather was *"perfect, the economy was great, and her family was there"*.

However, integrating into the new community took time. Attending a US school for the first time, Cynthia was forced to negotiate around several new situations. She was a quiet, timid child and speaking and understanding a new language and accents was the first obvious hurdle to overcome. She was also a *"little bit scared to open up to a lot of people because it's so different the way they talk"*. But language complications were merely the beginning. There were other little nuances of this new culture that seemed difficult to understand. One of these challenges was understanding the American culture of *"talking back"* to your school teachers. In Zimbabwe, the culture was that teachers were listened to and respected. It was a completely different environment in Texas, *"like apples and oranges"*.

The other issue for Cynthia was that she was the only Zimbabwean (or Black) student attending the Texan school and her first day certainly made an impression on her! Though the school she attended was in a good neighbourhood, on her very first day attending the school, somebody was stabbed. She spent much of the day hiding in the library, terrified that this might be just a normal day in an American school! When she finally got home after that eventful and seemingly endless first day, her brother asked her the customary, *"so did you have a good time at school today?"*. She replied, *"ahh no!"*. She was pretty scared to return the next day, but she did, and things did improve. The school managed the situation well and it never happened again. But *"it was just crazy that that was my first experience, my first day at an American school!"*.

While at secondary school, Cynthia did not develop the confidence to talk freely to many of the people around her. Partly this was due to the 'upfront' way that Cynthia thought many people talked to each other. Cynthia retells this story to illustrate the mixed messages she often received during this early period of adjustment.

Cynthia recalled one male student who would continually *"pick"* on her:

> *He would just walk in class and just throw out African jokes. . . . I ignored it and one day it was around prom time. I'm standing at the parking lot waiting for my brother to pick me up from school. From nowhere he comes out—this cute guy actually and to this day that was the weirdest—the first thing he says, 'hey Cynthia, can you go to the prom with me?' You could tell he was nervous.*
>
> *Of course, me out of nervousness, I was like 'no' [laughs] Poor thing he just walked away.*
>
> *Then actually I went to the prom without a date. I said no actually but I really wanted to [laughs]. He went by himself too. So, when I went back for a ten-year reunion after high school, and we started laughing about it. He said, 'yes, I did like you'.*

Perhaps just a normal case of terrified teenager nerves but Cynthia often sheeted these events back to her 'differentness' from everyone else and being on the quiet side. Academically she was powering along, leaving high school a year ahead of time to go to college. She was *"pumped"*, anticipating the career and life ahead. But life was about to change dramatically. Cynthia met a man she described as *"an idiot", but fell for him nevertheless and "skipped class and then fell pregnant"*. Whatever feelings she may have had for the father of her child, her plan of pursuing and developing a career definitely hit a roadblock. Cynthia left college and spent several years *"going to work, figuring out my budget and dealing with the stress of being a single mum"*.

With on-going family support and several years to take stock, Cynthia's plans were eventually back on track again. Her mother stayed close to Cynthia through the next few stages of her life. She flew to Texas and stayed with her there to help her look after her son while she did four years of nursing school. Then preferring to look after him in her home country, she returned to Zimbabwe with her grandson to enable Cynthia to have time to focus on completing her degree. She financed her nursing training from a full-time job in the insurance industry and by the time she had finished nursing school, her son was five years old and returned to live with her in the US.

But it didn't take long before Cynthia started to feel the need to move on . . . somewhere. It was around this time that a little seed had started to plant itself in her mind about moving to a country *"far away from her family where they can't call me"*. Cynthia decided early on in her nursing career that nursing would be a career that would provide her with challenges. She thought that if a nurse was unhappy that was their fault. *"What the heck is your problem? Nursing is such a vast occupation. If you hate something move on, go somewhere or do something. So, we vowed never to get bored."*

That's why she came to Australia.

Cynthia decided that what she needed at that moment was to create a new challenge. She immediately searched the internet and weighed up her options. Remember the plan was always to change things up *"so you don't get bored"*. Two months after the seed was planted to obtain an overseas posting, a recruitment agency was visiting her hospital and she booked an interview with the agency. At that meeting the recruiters slammed a map on the table in front of her and asked her: *"what are your preferences?"*. Looking blankly at this huge continent the only thing she could think to say was she, *"didn't want to work in the country"* and she, *"didn't want to do paper churning"*.

Cynthia did have some other issues on her wish list apart from an urban hospital and limited administration tasks. She wanted to work in a challenging nursing environment with modern equipment, with computerised systems and she wanted to continue working in her much-loved specialty area in a bone marrow unit.

With these criteria in mind, she also consulted friends to help decide where the best country to work might be. Several of Cynthia's friends had warned her that Australia could be a racist country, so they advised that she choose an urban area in which to work and live.

> *So, they were like if you go to Melbourne or Sydney it's a little bit okay because it's more diverse. So yes, but I was like okay so Sydney it is. The recruiter lays the map on the table and points to St Vincent's Hospital in central Sydney that included a large bone marrow transplant unit.*

It was less than a week later that an email arrived from St Vincent's Hospital containing a job offer.

The email and the prospect of moving to Sydney *"freaked"* Cynthia *"out"*. Her best friend advised her at the time: *""don't do it Cynthia!"*. Not being completely sure that she was doing the right thing, she kept pushing back the job offer to delay and further delay. However, eventually she signed the four-year 457 visa-sponsored contract with St Vincent's Hospital in Sydney.

But one month after she had arrived in Australia, she was feeling like she *"wanted to die. . . . I was like what have I done?"*.

New Frontiers and Saying Goodbye

The flight over the Australian continent is always a sobering reality check of the huge distance and space it covers. Cynthia was excited. Sitting beside her on the plane was her now-ten-year-old son. She felt apprehensive but also excited.

At that point she felt confident that the job would be fine. What worried her more was whether her son would be happy and settled. But all did not go well. On arrival at the airport they were picked up with their seven suitcases and driven to their hotel near Darling Harbour. When Cynthia arrived at her hotel, tears began to well up in her eyes:

> *I was like, 'what? What have I done?'. I was so depressed. I was trying not to be because my son, he's looking like, 'mum what is it?'. Then we get to the hotel, it's like a hiding area. It's like a—I can't explain it, it's just hiding. And I was just like, 'what the hell, this is supposed to be in the middle of the city!'.*
>
> *Yes, I'm like, 'oh my gosh' and my heart is just beating and the recruiter is trying to be upbeat. She's like, 'so what do you think?'. I was like, 'it's dirty' [laughs]. I was pissed [laughs]. She's like, 'actually most people say Sydney is the cleanest city in the world!'*

Cynthia's first day in Sydney was not as she had hoped it would be. Her expectations and dreams seemed poles apart from the reality of that day.

When Cynthia tried to check into her hotel, her credit card failed to process the payment for the room. Laden with bags and with her son beside her, Cynthia set off to the nearest ATM to withdraw AUD\$400 cash to pay for the hotel room. By the time she staggered to bed that night she was crying, wondering what she had done and whether this was a very big mistake.

Waiting several days to attain her registration to commence work, Cynthia tried to acclimatise to the new environment. But her son was not happy. He grumbled:

> *mum, it's cold here and there's too much water so if I fall in the water I could just die.*
>
> *I'm like dude, what are you even thinking? He's just like, 'I don't like it'.*
>
> *So, I bribe him with treats. I take him to McDonald's every morning, which I would have never normally done, but I was like, I'll do it for him. So, it was always McDonald's and he would get the toys and stuff and it was pretty rough.*
>
> *He got to the point after a week he was like, 'I hate it, I hate it, I want to go back home. I don't know why I'm here!'.*
>
> *So, I had to make the decision. It was hard, but he was unhappy. I had to pay AUD\$3,000 for a flight straight back to Texas for him.*

It goes without saying that the last thing that Cynthia wanted to do was say goodbye to her son, but she knew that he was unhappy in Sydney and there was little choice but to send him back to the US.

She also realised that it would be very difficult looking after him while she was working shifts including a morning shift one day, evening shift another, and all night shifts the next. This didn't seem to be clearly stated in her contract. But the unit manager advised *"well you didn't read it right because that's how nursing is in Australia. If you don't want it then you can catch a plane home"*.

With shifts like this, what would she do with her son?

> *I'm not going to let my son sleep on his own! So, the day care, work schedule pissed me off because he was like, '"Well if you can't do the rotating shift then we'll just give the position to someone else"'. In my head I'm like, "I just flew from here, I spent almost \$7,000 coming here!".*

Another issue that she hadn't thought of was the exorbitant cost of day care which turned out to be much more expensive than she had anticipated it would be. Cynthia's world started to unravel as she stressed about how work and family would tear each other apart and how lonely life would be without her son. As one little frustration mounted upon another, her challenges increased. The first month after her son had returned to Texas was definitely the worst period that Cynthia faced in Australia. That first year she felt that work was a small detail compared to finding a good place to live and coping with all of the expectations and loneliness that she experienced outside of work.

For example, the flat-sharing that she saw around her was completely foreign to her. It took her a long time to understand how Sydney residents coped with high house rentals. Her work colleague advised her:

> *You have to flatshare, that's how it is. I was like what if they kill me or rape me, or whatever? I don't know those people and she was like 'no, no, no that's how it is here'. She's like, 'come to my apartment I have three people that I live with and you'll see what I mean'. So, I go see and I'm like okay it looks okay. So, I start looking for a share apartment and found one within a month.*

But the workplace could also be a source of confusion at times. Clinical procedures were not the same in Australia as they were in the US such as information relating to medications, doctors' notes and care plans. In Australia, nurses dispense medications rather than have the pharmacy involved. This was a source of much anxiety for Cynthia because she was not told where to get the medicines and the medication names were often different in Australia. She felt embarrassed asking other nurses for help when she became confused about the many new processes she had to learn. Another nursing practice Cynthia was bemused and confused by was allowing patients to temporarily wander out of the hospital by themselves. She recalled:

> *You can't do that in America [laughs]. I freaked out. They're like, well he's going to go out for a smoke and go have lunch. I was like what if he has a seizure out there and he just folds up. Ah it's fine that's just how it is here. So, you can't—all those things were throwing me out, I'm like, 'oh my gosh!'. But anyway, I'm getting used to it. I'm just like, I guess if they fall out there, they'll call frigging 911 [laughs] somebody will come.*

Nursing in bone marrow units offered Cynthia autonomy and job quality. This was an area of nursing that she felt challenged her and which she has always loved:

> *Bone marrow was more caring because you actually get two or three patients at the most. You get more leeway on the bone marrow unit*

*because they teach you more . . . you're doing a lot by yourself, just
thinking by yourself.*

The pace and connection in bone marrow is something that Cynthia remarks
on regularly. She compares it to other areas of nursing where you have little
time to connect with patients because you are expected to *"run, run, run"*.

*In bone marrow you've got three patients. You walk in, sit down. You
ask what's going on. Then you talk, they vent, and you say, 'okay well
this is what I understand is going on today and this is what I think
I'm going to be doing for you. So, tell me if there is anything else that
you might have forgotten to tell the doctor that I can help you with'....
'Yes, I think I've a mouth ulcer.'... 'Okay, let me look at it. Okay I'm
going to swab it. Okay cool. I'm going to give you this', and we'll do
that, you know. So, you actually get to sit there and talk and do more
instead of just run, run, run. So, I love that, and you develop relationships with them. It's sad that some of them die but you literally—you
develop relationships. You can actually care for them and see the
results right away.*

There is also the sense that patients are committed to their own recovery.
As she laments:

*In medical surgery patients might arrive with high blood sugar because
they ate too much cake and they come back next week with the same
problem [laughs]. They are more frustrating because they don't care.
It's frustrating because you're sitting there, hey you're on an insulin
drip and the family sneaks in a bag of hot wings. You're like, 'seriously
what are you doing?'.*

Losing patients was initially very hard to deal with. Cynthia thought there
was something wrong with her:

*I know it's weird. Seriously, patients would die. I will hold them and I'll
be rubbing the back of the family members. Like, it's okay. We all die.
My mindset is okay I'm glad they are resting they fought a good battle.
So, I mean I've done it all this time and I've always wondered what is
wrong with me? Should I be crying?*

Like many other nurses, Cynthia could form strong attachments to some
of her patients, but one patient stood out. She had worked five straight shifts
in what was to be the last week in one young patient's life.

On the last night that he was dying I was crying like a baby. The mum was sitting at his bedside and saying, 'you fought a good battle, I just want you to know I love you'.

Usually I can stand there and just be like, 'oh you're so right'. I was just like [makes crying sound]. I had tissues and I'm looking for Visine. I'm like—because I don't want to be the nurse crying and then the mum said something like, 'oh I just want you to know that you've been the best nurse ever to him' and—the night before she didn't spend the night with him and I had to. It's like, 'thank you for being his mother last night' and I was just like [makes crying sound]. I'm like, 'ahh this is horrible'. But I'm close friends with the family now.

Being 'here', Back and Forward

It took Cynthia a good year after she arrived in Australia to start to feel comfortable and possibly even settled. In many ways Cynthia feels that she has achieved what she had set out to achieve and learnt a lot professionally along the way. Reflecting on time in Australia she feels that, while professional integration had come relatively easily, social integration was much more problematic, noting that most of her workmates and friends are also migrants from other countries.

Her feeling towards migration and her nursing work has changed during the time she has been in Australia:

Now I'm good. Before if you met me, my plan was to literally finish this year and go back. I was like, yes, I'll keep touring Australia like I've been doing and go back. But now I'm good. The other day I was thinking I remembered when I talked to my sister and she irritated me so bad. Then I was like, 'Oh my gosh! This is what I prayed for, freedom!'. I was like I don't even have to tell her where I am. I was like, 'Cynthia you're forgetting'—because you get so caught up in the stress that you're real. Okay God has given me this. I've always wanted to travel, and I've travelled—but I couldn't because I had a kid. Then I was like, I've been here literally seven months. I've been on a plane almost every month travelling different places than I've ever done in my whole entire life. So, then I think I'm getting that epiphany of 'Oh my gosh! Enjoy it and just chill out!'. So that's why now I'm like, okay I'm open-minded. I'm in no hurry to go back home. Home is always there.

Like all migrants, Cynthia retains very strong ties to her home country, Zimbabwe. Her father passed away ten years ago, and her mother and two siblings work in Zimbabwe after managing to secure employment in Harare.

There are now mixed opportunities for her friends and family in Zimbabwe:

> *Being Zimbabwean, the goal was to go overseas and get educated then you can actually go back home because things would get better. But now, things went south so [laughs] no! But the weird part is the people that are doing great, are doing really great in Zimbabwe. There is no middle class, it's kind of like, you're either doing really good or you're doing really bad. So, my brother he runs a Toyota company there. I think he's been with that company a long time, so they provide a house, car, the company, all that stuff. So, he's doing pretty well for himself.*

Throughout her life, Cynthia has heavily depended on church associations to make social connections. It is this deep spiritual connection that finds Cynthia wanting to 'give back'. After several years working and living in Australia therefore, Cynthia is again looking to her future. *"I want a challenge, I want to make a difference in the world. I know I'm nursing, but I think I need to do more. So, part of me is yearning, I want to go back to Zimbabwe to help the young kids there."*

Her sister has become heavily involved in an entrepreneurial charity that has become very successful at raising money for Zimbabwean families. There is an ironic coincidence here. Growing up, Cynthia claims that her sister was always a hoarder. This is a trait that is now helping others. This sister has suggested to all the members of the family who live overseas that instead of donating their clothes to American charity shops, they collect their used clothing and ship them back to Zimbabwe.

> *She bought a container filled it up with all those clothes and shoes and shipped it to my mum. My mum just got it three weeks ago. She's selling those clothes like five bucks each. I think she's making money like that [clicks fingers]. People are buying clothes like, oh you got this from America? And these are really good clothes. My sister's like 'see you don't even have to send mum pocket money because she's making more than the bank' [laughs].* [She is saying that instead of giving clothes to local charities she sends the clothes to Zimbabwe.]

Activities like these augment the AUD$250 monthly remittances that Cynthia has regularly sent back to her mother ever since she left Zimbabwe. Indeed, these remittances have allowed her mother to employ a maid!

Now the containers of clothes are being supplemented with containers of non-perishable food and household items including rice, canned beans, soap, dishwashing liquid. Soon Cynthia will join her sister in Zimbabwe for a month to help the family sell and distribute these items.

Cynthia is keen to visit and 'go back' to Zimbabwe. *"I'm like okay next vacation let me go to Africa for a month and take off from there, yes. So, it's like back and forth."*

Over the years, Cynthia has had a great family support network. Even though at times she wanted to run a mile from that, she knows that she has heavily relied on their close support.

> *She reminded herself a couple of days ago—just being Christian I just prayed. I was like God, I want a challenge, I want to make a difference in the world, I know I'm doing the nursing, but I think I need to do more. So, part of me is yearning, I want to go back to Zimbabwe to the young kids with what my sister did with the clothes. I want to go to orphanages and take clothes there. If I can get my friends just to buy an outfit for each girl or boy and once a year, I'll go with new outfits and shoes. I think that'll be awesome. Anyway, so that's my little goal. Also help as far as medication if I can get somebody to work with me. That's why I also hooked up with the African Women's Association.*

Cynthia's plan was always do something different. *"My friends are now married. They have bought homes and stuff and I'm like, I'm 30 what else is next, have a kid. I mean I can go to school and get my Master's which I can do while I'm travelling but what else? Remember the plan was to always change up things so you don't get bored."*

But she often faced tensions balancing her work and family commitments. A tension between her desire to leave and be free and her desire to be happy and stable. But at the moment she feels that she has struck a good balance between these important aspirations. Her latest plan is to lure her son back to Australia by posting enticing photos of the Whitsunday Islands, the Hunter Valley and Cairns on Facebook. She has an ultimatum for him though, which is that if he comes back to Australia, he must stay for at least one year, *"even if it gets . . . bad or anything you're just going to have to push through it because you can't just move"*. He's like, *"okay"*. I said, *"you'll only have one week off and we'll go straight into school"*.

When she said these words, we wondered whether her son would be able to do what she had done. Remember the plan was always to change things up so you don't get bored!

Note

1. Gaidzanwa, R. B. (1999). *Voting with their Feet: Migrant Zimbabwean Nurses and Doctors in the Era of Structural Adjustment* (No. 11). Nordic Africa Institute.

6   Sheila

Don't Think About Why
You *Can't Do*, Think About
How You *Can Do*!

Introduction

Sheila has worked for many years as an Education Manager, where she has coordinated the learning needs of the nursing staff at one of the largest private hospitals in north Sydney. Her job involves managing the mandatory training and education programmes required for the hospital's accreditation status. Thus, while the job requires close working relationships with managers in order to coordinate the accreditation process, she keeps a very close eye on the learning needs of recently graduated nurses whom she selects in the recruitment rounds. As such, Sheila spends much of her time educating young students about the daily aspects of nursing and health care.

This role is particularly important in the context of tertiary nurse training. The induction to, and immersion in, the reality of ward nursing is something Sheila recognises as very important to nurse training and effective workplace integration. She recognises that others—particularly the older generation of nurses—can be critical of tertiary-trained nurses; less experienced than those that have learnt on-the-job. However, she also believes that contemporary nursing has fundamentally changed from when she trained as a nurse during the 1980s. Part of the problem from Sheila's perspective is that while the transition from hospital to tertiary training was a positive development, few structures are put in place that support nurse graduates in their first year of working in a hospital system.

The importance of acculturating nurses into the hospital environment has always been an issue very close to Sheila's professional heart. This strong sense of professional development was also reflected in a desire to emphasise how the patient's view of nursing might be changing. These two priorities of nurse training and patient-centred care have shaped Sheila's professional priorities and her journey. Sheila noted:

> *Imagine a patient is angry or shouting at a nurse. How would they deal with that? One of the things we do not want to hear, if they are in that sort of situation, is: 'well I told them not to speak to me like that'. Of course, we do not want nurses to be threatened, but most patients in this environment are scared and anxious and in pain; people are worried about their loved ones. So we need nurses to help try and soothe that and diffuse it and understand all those aspects that are making the patient or family member behave that way.*

Being 'there' and Not Being Left Behind

From as far back as she can remember, Sheila always wanted to follow in her mother's footsteps and become a nurse. Her mother was born in Ireland but she had completed her nurse training on the Isle of Man. After she met Sheila's father, she moved to England. Sheila's father worked for the army so the family moved around a lot, travelling throughout England as well as to Hong Kong. Sheila is the youngest of three children, alongside two older brothers.

Sheila was very young when she became aware of the type of work her mother did. She would often visit her mother at work and watch her during her shifts at the aged care facility at which she worked. *"I used to love going there and sitting with the old ladies and they would always give me 10p. They were just gorgeous and so thrilled to spend time with somebody."* Sheila liked the interpersonal aspects of the work and she also had a strong sense that she wanted to do something similar to her mum that was *"really helpful"*.

As Sheila matured, she realised that nursing was a very versatile career. While her mother had become a nurse because there were few other options in Ireland in the 1940s, one generation on, Sheila had more options—yet nursing won out in the end. She dreamt about being a singer or a horse rider or a secretary, because she *"loved stationery"* and being organised.

Sheila knew enough about nursing from following her mother around. She knew it wasn't a glamorous career. She knew it was hard work and that the hours were long and that she would be required to work night shifts, holidays and Christmas Day when family occasions would be missed. She also knew that she would be confronted with sick patients, and that she would have occasions when she would not be able to make them better.

After talking with a careers counsellor at the college she attended after completing high school, she applied directly to nursing schools. She secured a place at The John Radcliffe Hospital in Oxford. The first time she entered the hospital for the interview left a strong impression on her:

> *I can remember my dad took me for the interview. I was 17 and we drove to Oxford and I'd never seen a place like it in my life and I just remember saying to my dad, 'I want to come here!'. Then we drove up to the hospital on top of the hill and it was this big white modern tiled amazing looking building. I was just awestruck—it was massive and I just thought, just get me in there!*

During the 1980s, nurse training was hospital-based rather than university-based. The three-year nursing programme commenced with six weeks of in-class learning, involving various aspects of anatomy, physiology, followed by an eight-week placement in a local hospital working with patients in a variety of areas including aged care and paediatrics in the first year. What followed was oncology and the intensive care unit, emergency, and other critical care areas. After Sheila graduated and qualified as a registered nurse in 1985, she spent another year at the hospital before she acted on her desire to work in cardiac and coronary care.

Her first move involved working in neighbouring Cambridge, allocated to a general ward in a large hospital. When she mentioned she was *interested in the heart*, her manager encouraged her to ask at the coronary care ward if there were any positions available. Thus began her career in coronary care where she would remain for a decade and a half. Sheila's work in coronary care took her to regional hospitals in towns such as Liverpool, and then Nottingham, followed by a six-month coronary care course and a move to Bath. In the span of six years, Sheila lived and worked in five different locations! These relatively easy transitions reflect the buoyancy of the nursing labour market during the early 1990s.

Part of the reason Sheila gives for moving around so much was her desire to 'grow up', and not wanting to be 'left behind'. She was keen to develop her professional responsibility and the fact that many of her friends were getting married, settling down and moving away hastened her desire to also actively seek out change. She looked back at this period and reflected how she tried to spearhead activities that would offer change. Perhaps a fear of being left behind, both professionally and personally was starting to envelop her?

While she was working in Bath, Sheila had it within her sights to move into a management role within coronary care. However, securing a management position within this area of nursing in those days was "*literally like waiting for people to die*". Highly prized positions would rarely be given up. After having been based in Bath for nine years, Sheila began to look further afield. She applied for a number of manager positions and was successful in obtaining one at a hospital in Bristol. However, the job meant that she had to leave her beloved area of coronary care for a general medical ward. After a year in the position she happened to be chatting on the phone to a friend with whom she had trained in Oxford who was at the time living in Sydney. Sheila mentioned to her that she was planning a holiday in January 2000 and was thinking of going to Canada. The friend's immediate response was: "*What are you going to Canada for? It is freezing. Come to Australia!*"

Sheila set off on a three-week Australian holiday. On reflection she realises that this was a time of immense restlessness, both personal and professional. At the time Sheila was living alone. Furthermore, despite, or because of, the fact that she had moved around the country many times, she felt that she was going nowhere professionally, just working in the same job, day in, day out.

This period of self-reflection coincided with a family wedding where Sheila became involved in a conversation with her aunt Noreen who was a nun, but also a family therapist, academic and social worker. Sheila described her aunt as very learned and someone who had always answered those strange, tricky childhood questions. Sheila reflected on her curiosity about her aunt who *wore a habit and was married to God*. As an adult, her close ties with aunt Noreen were evident in what transpired to be one of the most influential conversations in her life. During that conversation, Sheila noted her desire to "*just go and do something really different; go and travel abroad.* As Sheila recalls:

> I had obviously had a big debrief with her—which I could not remember an awful lot about by the end of the night. But she rang me up about three weeks later and said 'oh I wondered if you had thought any more about what you were saying'. I said, 'oh no not really'. I said, 'I just feel like I can't, because what am I going to do with my flat, and like, I would miss the nephews and nieces if I went away. How would I do this?'. She said, 'Oh they are all really valid points, but I think you have to think about how you can do it!'.

It was almost like the penny dropped. I will sell my flat then. I will get a job out there, and I will go and do that. It was almost instantaneous. It was an amazing thing, and I often say that to people now. I use that phrase—don't think about why you can't, think about how you can— and it just completely turned it around for me.

It turned out that this motto of being positive and decisive became quite a mantra for Sheila. Much of her approach to her personal and professional development involved her taking personal responsibility for making things work, or rather making things work better, or finding new ways to solve a problem. At that point in time Sheila had ended a romantic relationship and was living very close to her extended family. She was at the time 'Aunty Sheila' doing a lot of babysitting and wondering whether *"this could be it. . . . Do I want to be doing this in ten years' time?"*.

Being ' in-between'

Sheila took a short trip to Australia where she had scaled the heights and breadth of the country by visiting Central Australia and Uluru, South Australia and the Barossa Valley as well as Sydney. Thinking she would never return she felt she had covered a lot of ground in a short space of time. After arriving back in the UK however, Sheila found herself thinking a lot about Australia. There was no doubt in her mind that she loved Sydney. But it wasn't just the beautiful location, she was wondering what she was doing with her life, where she was going and why she was feeling so restless.

She began to investigate the prospect of securing a nursing job in Sydney. It was the year 2000 and Sheila scoured *The Nursing Times* to see what jobs were being advertised by the many international recruitment agencies. She easily found several job opportunities in Sydney, one in particular involved working in a high-dependency unit at the Mater Hospital in North Sydney. Sheila thought the position could be interesting and she felt positive about the prospects of her future in a new country.

The wheels were now in motion. She secured the four-year employment sponsorship and then set out to 'close a few doors' deciding to sell her apartment, put her things in storage and head to Australia. She was determined not to make it too easy to opt out of the challenges she was setting up for herself by returning home to her cosy apartment. She was determined not to, *"come back to the same thing"*. Sheila saw the freedom of ridding herself of material possessions that might undermine her determination to start something new. Flush with the money from the sale of her apartment, Sheila went shopping before she left the UK:

buying things and not worrying about it. I went to Marks & Spencer and bought the best. Yeah, I treated myself and I remember buying things that I didn't actually need. So I'd buy myself a necklace and it had my birthstone in it and I'm thinking, oh yeah, well I can just buy that. It was a really nice time. I was 34—and I suppose I wasn't doing bad. I had my own flat and I had a car and I had a good job.

Sheila had already done quite a bit of travel. She had travelled to Sweden, the Middle East, China, the US as well as many European countries. While Australia and the UK are assumed to be very similar in many ways, Sheila was to experience many challenges.

Being 'here': Living in Hostels and Working in Sacks

Having owned her own apartment and lived in comfort, Sheila was not completely prepared for the living and working conditions awaiting her in Australia. She arrived in Australia on a Thursday and started work the following Monday. She described this experience with a heavy clarity. She spent the first four to six weeks thinking:

What have I done? What have I done? It was just culturally more different than I thought it was going to be. Starting as a new person in a new hospital in a new country, my first day, I can remember the uniforms didn't fit me; they were massive, so I felt like a right idiot just wearing this sack. My first day on the ward, the nurse that was supposed to be looking after me, said, 'oh well, are you happy to take a patient load?'. I said, 'No, I am not. This is my first day in this hospital in this country. I do not think it would be very safe.' She said, 'oh well, you better go and read those folders then'.

The folders the senior nurse was referring to contained the policies and procedures of the hospital. While Sheila was given a more formal hospital orientation a week later, throughout her first day she felt she was relegated to read manuals and observe from the sidelines in her new ill-fitting 'sack'. In some respects, Sheila was a little out of her depth. Her preference for coronary care and medical ward, meant that it had been 15 or 16 years since she had experienced surgical nursing. Additionally, she was using pumps she had never seen; infusions she was unfamiliar with; wound drains she had never worked with before; and a whole new language in terms of the way people spoke about medical procedures, medications and patients. For example, references to the DDs—Dangerous Drugs—described dangerous drugs of addiction like morphine and pethidine in the UK. In Australia these drugs were called S8—Schedule 8 medications. Thus, when a colleague asked her whether she had counted the S8s, she was completely bewildered. During this initial stage of her employment in Australia, it seemed she was left to fend for herself with little orientation and support that she values so much today.

Cultural nuances and phrases she experienced outside work were also perplexing. Bank accounts are called different things in the UK. EFTPOS was an unfamiliar term, and the lack of insider knowledge made her feel like an 'idiot':

> *So you have all these kinds of episodes that you know probably just knock your confidence a bit. You think, oh we speak the same language it can't be that hard. But yes there were quite a few episodes in the early days. But you learn so much from that. You learn so much about being new and what it feels like for people. I think it has really helped me.*

Social aspects of her work also took some getting used to:

> *That was the other interesting thing—where I worked in England, if we had a new staff member join us, it would be 'great, let's go on a night out, let's all do something'. That evolved later but it didn't evolve as quickly as I thought. I thought nursing is fine because people will say, 'come on, you are new, let's go out'. That didn't happen. So that was a quite a difference for me. I do not know whether that is because I went to a private hospital and the culture there was a bit different. I mean I have not worked in a public hospital in Australia. Or it might have been the age of the group of nurses that were there. They were a bit older, and that did evolve and I ended up being good friends with some of those people, but in the initial weeks no one said, 'Oh you must come round and have dinner'. That was the sort of thing I thought will be a lifesaver. So I would go back to the hostel where I was staying and get on the email and just sit there crying; thinking I must be crazy, what am I doing?*

In addition to the lack of social interaction and initiatives to include a new member of staff, her living arrangements were also challenging her decision:

> *My room was horrible, my curtains were torn and hanging off the rails, the walls were filthy, bed old and uncomfortable and traffic noise was like living on the road (which may have been preferable and cheaper). After I had managed to find the bathroom myself (I wasn't guided around the big building at all), had a shower (after I had scared away*

> a cockroach [please don't think I am making this up]) and went to use
> the toilet, however I had to find another toilet as this one had (human,
> I presume) excrement all over it, that is over it NOT in it.

The hostel facility was definitely targeting students and while cheap, it
was quite a shock for Sheila who had gone from living in a comfortable
one-bedroom apartment in Bath to having a poorly maintained room with a
shared kitchen and a bathroom in various states of disrepair.

The hostel did however provide occasional moments of social interaction.
Sheila remembers forcing herself one evening to go downstairs and join the
sea of faces in the communal kitchen. After collecting her dinner and seeing
some stethoscopes on the table, she ended up spending an enjoyable evening with several medical students. She also became aware of another UK
nurse staying at the hostel and the two became instant friends, subsequently
moving into an apartment together. This put Sheila in a much better frame
of mind and this was a big turning point. With a nice apartment with a view
of the Harbour Bridge, things were looking up.

Being 'here' and Getting 'there'

Sheila was initially reluctant to commit to living in Australia for the full four
years. She had in her mind that moving to Australia for a year would change
her path and make her forge a new direction. She saw the move as a stepping-
stone to a direction she was not sure of but a moment in time away that she
needed. But by 2002, six months led to one year and then two years, and after
Sheila had completed two years of the contract, she applied for permanent
residency. A month later she met a *"nice chap"* who went on to become her
husband. The workplace also started to become more interesting as Sheila went
from having a Clinical Nurse Specialist role to an education role, as a Cardiac Educator. Work was certainly keeping her challenged; as was the master's
degree she undertook. But she began again to wonder what to do next.

Compared to the colleagues with whom she graduated, Sheila describes
herself as a *"late developer"*. She thinks it took her a lot of time both as
a nurse and as a person to push herself and undertake further study. Many
of her friends had completed specialist courses in areas such as intensive
care in the first year or two after qualification. By contrast, Sheila did not
complete her coronary care course until four or five years later. She also
went back to complete her A level in English as well as a Bachelor's degree.
Possibly overly critical of her achievements, Sheila feels that it has taken her
a long time to 'get there', having only just completed her Master's degree.

Most of the nurses Sheila trained with are no longer in the nursing
profession. There are even fewer who have remained in acute hospital

environments. For Sheila though, she still gets a *"bit of a buzz"* when she walks into a hospital. She highlights that nursing has provided for a great career and it has given her many opportunities:

> *I remember as a child thinking 'oh I would not want to live if I lost a toe! You have those really stupid thoughts, and then nursing helps you put everything into perspective. You know you think you are having a bad day, but actually you are going home at the end of the day and you see parents walk out and their child has died; you develop these amazing friendships. Like my eight, nine, ten years in coronary care, they were some of the best years of my life because I was an expert in that field. I knew it, and we had a great team of doctors who trusted us and we had a great team of nurses that worked so well together.*

In particular, coronary care has formed a strong scaffold around Sheila's enthusiasm for nursing. When she first started in the field, coronary care was a life and death situation where massive heart attacks led inevitably to severely damaged heart muscles. There was also the added potential for serious and difficult complications and often loss of life. This situation led to much quality time spent with patients, (and their extended family) educating them about risk factors and healthy lifestyles. She welcomed the interaction with other nurses in the unit as well as the close interaction with the patients themselves. The hospital workplace still has appeal to Sheila many years after she first started nursing. She states: *"I love being in a hospital. Like I like the fact that my job is still in a hospital. I've always enjoyed that"*.

Taking Next Steps

Sheila's current position has taken her many miles from her initial nursing position in Sydney. Her new position requires that she review all clinical policies in a new private hospital in the Sunshine Coast, Queensland. This role takes her to familiar territory: that is, looking after the education and professional development of the nurses that will staff that hospital. Shaped by her own experience in those initial days in Sydney, she has initiated the introduction of an additional day for nurse orientation making sure that nurses know about hospital policy and how that plays out on a daily basis. During these orientations Sheila asks staff and students: *"What do you do when a new nurse arrives at the ward? We have all been in that situation where people look away and look busy, and I am saying to them: 'how about, hello, who are you, and do you know where to sit?'"*.

Sheila seems, as always, to be very happy in her new role. However, there is also a little restlessness. She is reflecting on her next step professionally with customary optimism. *"Moving to a private corporation is an option. That would be a bit strange. But I am starting to see that, because I think that is the role I will have to look at to take my next step. But I do, I really like it here."*

There is also the matter of her strong personal links with her home country. Having recently turned 50, her mind seems to take her back to the UK more often. Her parents and her two brothers and their wives had recently visited Australia for a month. She felt that her brothers were now more like friends—as they all *"got on"* and she missed her extended family and long-term friends. She also reflected on her mother's ailing health while discussing how her father was still running around like a *"spring chicken"*. After her family returned to the UK, she thought more about what the next phase of her life might look like.

It is very clear that nursing has been the perfect career for Sheila:

> *For me nursing has been a great career and it has given me a lot of opportunities, and when I think about the experiences I have had with people—which is what I suppose made me want to go into nursing—it has absolutely given me everything. You learn so much about people and you learn so much about life that you carry it over to your own life.*
>
> *This is going to sound a bit out there, but I want to be able to inspire people. I think I have got a lot of experience now and I have learnt a lot about people and communication and managing situations and that is what I think I would love to be: leading a team. I think I have got all that experience—because you never stop learning of course—but I see so many episodes of poor leadership that I feel like I think I would have something to offer there.*

A Life and Career in Reflection

Sheila feels that there are three options in the nursing profession. Burnout might come from working in the fast-paced and physically demanding and stressful psychological and emotional environment of an emergency department. Then there is rust-out, where you have no stimulation in your work, just sitting there waiting for the time to tick over. Then there is the third option of finding new directions. Sheila chose the last option.

Sheila is the only nurse in this book who migrated from an English-speaking country with a relatively similar cultural heritage. Despite these similarities, Sheila faced numerous challenges. While English is our common language there remain many differences in how people communicate with each other both in and outside the workplace. The challenges Sheila faced were difficult for her, however she also recognises how they also instilled self-reliance and an acute intuition to make things better for future nurses. She feels proud of herself for opening up her world to new experiences.

Sheila has also admired what she observes of the Australian nursing workforce. She stated that: *"Nurses aren't afraid of hard work, staying late and getting the job done"*. She feels they have an immense practicality about nursing practice:

> *If I came across a new dressing, for example, and it was a bit compli-cated, I would be like, 'Oh God!'. Whereas I could guarantee the Aussie nurse would say, 'well where's the instructions—alright, well let's get everything we need. Okay, well let's have a go.'. Within the realms of professionalism—as in I have a bit of an idea about what I'm doing. I understand the process, but this is a new dressing. Yeah I think that's exactly it. I think it is that 'getting in and having a go' sort of attitude—and make the best of it. That's what I saw a lot of.*

Sheila knows that you can achieve a lot just by *"being kind to people and it's alright to be honest, as long as you do it with really good intentions and you do it from a place of kindness"*. This empathy was a common theme in Sheila's working life. She felt that more needed to be done to welcome new nurses into the workplace. As she reflected:

> *when I was younger and you joined a workplace, it was 'oh we're going on a night would you like to come along?'. So when a new nurse starts work she organises a night out to get to know them. . . . I remember saying to my friends in England when I was leaving for Australia: 'I'll be fine—I'm a nurse—it's a nursing job—people will ask me to go out. But when I got here, nobody did!'. I remember one day I got really badly bitten by mosquitoes and I'd gone into work with massive welts when I first came out here. The next day one of the girls brought me an aloe-vera plant and said, 'oh you should rub this on your skin'. I thought it was a really lovely thing to do, but she still didn't invite me around for a cup of tea.*

Migrant workers often feel like outsiders, particularly in those first few years of living in Australia. This is the case regardless of their country of origin. Sheila has, over time, built a very rewarding career and social net-work and feels that she has settled happily in Australia. However, she has overcome many challenges to get to this position and the forces drawing her back to her homeland remain strong.

7 Pinky

From the Philippines to Sydney and Back

Introduction

The Philippines has a rich and long history of nurse migration. This history highlights the way that ethnicity, gender and class shape the transnational nursing labour force. For many years, nurses, and other citizens seeking a viable living in other counties have remitted vast amounts of funds to the Philippine economy. Pinky, like many before her, and many to follow her in the future—left her country, her husband and her young children to search for work in a bid to provide for her family back home.

Pinky knows that her life in Australia is a far stretch from her childhood and youth in the regional southern provinces of the Philippines. As a young woman, she had no grand plans to live overseas, however the path that emerged before her provided her with this well-trodden route. Given her country's history of exporting nurses into the global health industry, Pinky felt that there was a good chance that she would leave the country at some point in her life. As we speak, Pinky talks about the twists and turns her life has taken in a slightly melancholy but resigned way. Pinky has learnt to 'go with the flow'. Her decisions often seem to be made in the context of how they affect others, particularly her children, her husband and her parents. There seems a clear practicality and inevitability about the direction in which she will go. When asked how many years she has lived away from her children while working overseas, she replied:

> *it's been a long time, but it's not just me you know. It's a hard life in the Philippines, it's common for a family—one family member—to be away and work. I know we have the consequences, the negative effect of that. But it's practical for us really. It's just we need to survive. I know we have choices but it's us, we don't have a choice. We need to do it.*

Working thousands of miles from where her husband now lives and works, there is also an inevitability that this separation may continue for some time into the future. Her current employment has taken her a long way from the typhoon-prone regions of the Philippines where she grew up, to the east coast of New Zealand and now to Sydney where we meet today. She is clearly proud of her achievements so far and wears her uniform piously. Her life and career may not have turned out exactly as she had imagined, but her approach to life is both fatalistic and optimistic.

The word 'survival' surfaces a lot in conversations with Pinky. Perhaps this focus on survival results from the many natural disasters that she faced with her family as she was growing up. The typhoons, the storms and the need to rebuild is not far from her thoughts. However, her determination to not just survive but to thrive and flourish has given her the ability to put both of her two daughters through university in Australia: one in the area of nursing and the other in accounting. Pinky will tell you proudly that this is her finest achievement!

Being 'there'

At the age of 43, Pinky knows that her journey has not been easy, however, she also feels that she has lived a very fortunate life. She was born in 1972 in the southern region of the Philippines in Samar in a small town called San Jose. The coastal region may have been beautiful, but it was extremely under-developed and there were very few employment opportunities. Part of the reason that San Jose had such poor infrastructure was due to the extreme weather patterns that hit the area regularly. Most particularly, the area is subject to regular typhoons that would often destroy the local communities and limit the potential for significant investment. For example, in November 2013 Typhoon Melor killed 45 people in San Jose and left thousands without food, water and urgent medical care, and in December 2015 over 4,000 people died in the Philippines from Typhoon Haiya. Pinky recalls these events as regular and devastating.

The unpredictability in the weather patterns and poor infrastructure meant that most of the economic activities in the area were limited to fishing and farming. The living conditions growing up were tenuous and the employment prospects for children remaining in the area were limited. As a result, many young people living in San Jose had to leave the area to find work in Manila or migrate overseas if they had the resources to do so.

Pinky grew up with her mother, who was a registered midwife, and her father, a former priest in the Philippine Independent Church, which is a branch of the Catholic Church. Due to financial hardship her father left the priesthood and took up a job as a chef on a large transportation ship and has recently retired from this work. Both of Pinky's parents worked very hard and encouraged their three children, one boy and two girls, to follow their example.

Life in the Philippines revolved around largely farming activities. Given that there was four years difference in age between her siblings, Pinky doesn't recall much of her youth with them but does remember the year when she left home to live with her older brother and sister when they attended university in Manila. Boarding with them from the tender age of 12 opened the way for Pinky to attend a Catholic high school there, while her mother and father remained in San Jose.

During this period when Pinky went to school and her siblings went to university, five extended family members squashed into their two-bedroom Manila apartment. It was here that Pinky completed her high school years and then without seeming to give it a 'second thought', enrolled in a four-year nursing degree at United Doctors Medical Centre. Compared to alternative courses, such as accountancy or hotel management, nursing seemed a sensible choice. It gave Pinky good prospects for financial stability and the opportunity to travel overseas.

Studying nursing also brought Pinky and her future husband together, as he was studying at the same college. While the two married, the nursing life did not suit Pinky's husband, so he joined the family's construction business in the region where he was born, Claveria Cagayan. Like San Jose, this area is also coastal, but it is better resourced and due to the links to the Marcos family, considerable money had been invested in local infrastructure. There were also many more opportunities for important business connections to assist her husband's business there. Being the only child, the pressure to continue the family business was strong. However, this region was a long way from San Jose and Pinky had fewer opportunities there than those available to her in Manila.

Nevertheless, the couple moved to Claveria Cagayan and Pinky secured a part-time job as an occupational health and safety nurse in a local resort hotel. In 2000 she had her first daughter and then her second arrived two years later. Professionally however this was a period of some stagnation so

Pinky decided to move to the Agra Medical Centre where she also worked part-time between 2000 to 2008. Again, the job secured her continued registration and a nursing licence, but it offered few professional opportunities as more complex medical procedures were usually diverted to larger, better equipped hospitals elsewhere. In 2006, Pinky had her third child, this time a boy, and again work took second place to family responsibilities. Life continued on for some years; Pinky raised three children without much time or thought about work and career.

Being ' in-between'

Pinky does not describe herself as a planner, things *"just happen . . . I don't want to plan ahead for my future because I don't want to be frustrated when I don't get it"*. She talks about her life being lived on a, *"day-to-day basis . . . whatever comes. Okay I'm on my way. Because when my kids were growing up, I didn't have a plan. It was okay. It's just like surviving."*

But at some point, Pinky thought, *"I'm done with that"*. Pinky thought a lot about the future for her children and her family. With three growing children to look after she asks, *"What will happen to them?"*. Her reflection is also set within the context of the political situation in the Philippines at the time which meant that without connections in the government and the political process, business would be difficult to sustain: *"if you are not so close to politicians then you will have nothing. You will have no job."* A further complication is that, as the political composition changes with each election, the need to secure connections with locally elected officials is an ongoing necessity. Every three years there is potentially a new round of networks that need to be built up and maintained. Building a business in this context is a time-consuming process that takes years to cultivate. There is also a dark side to such a context—rife with nepotism and corruption, one's life is never truly secure.

While the opportunities for her husband may have been buoyed by the political situation at the time, the professional opportunities for Pinky were slowly slipping away and life felt like it was, *"standing still"*. While still working part-time at the Agra Medical Centre, Pinky completed several refresher courses that would prepare her for nursing work overseas. In 2008 she successfully passed the required test to gain a licence to work in California but there were no jobs (or visas) on offer due to the global financial crisis that saw eight million Americans lose their jobs. The lack of available positions in the US led Pinky to look southward to other countries and soon an opportunity to work arose in New Zealand.

Pinky had never heard of New Zealand: *"never in my life!"*. However, when she was offered a student visa to study for three months at the Bay of

Plenty—in Tauranga in the north island of New Zealand, she accepted the offer immediately.

Pinky arrived in New Zealand in the summer of 2009 with a group of other international students who undertook language studies at the Waikato University. She remembered the course fees to be roughly NZ$5,000 just for the processing fee and Pinky had to work 20 hours per week to finance these costs. It wasn't until November that she secured her first 'proper' job. She studied and worked at BUPA Health nursing home in Tauranga for ten months while her husband cared for their children in the Philippines. This period of Pinky's life presented a steep learning curve as she had limited experience in aged care and no experience of many of the psychotropic medications she was expected to administer to patients. This was an area of nursing that she had not been exposed to in her home country, but again the word survival springs to her mind, *"I have to do this to survive, for the kids, for the family"*.

In contrast to the Philippines, the work environment she faced in the aged care facility drove her to seek more interesting professional challenges. A side shift to Tauranga Public Hospital in 2011 partly satiated this desire to gain more expertise, greater skills and professional development, and more of what she describes as 'proper nursing'. The job also gave her access to modern equipment and training and support along the way, to help with undertaking blood transfusions and more complicated procedures than she had been exposed to in previous years.

However, meeting other Filipino nurses who were preparing to leave for positions in Australia got Pinky thinking of another shift, this time to Australia. Again, Pinky thought Australia would be *"a better place to raise children and the pay is higher"*. She therefore applied for work and quickly received a job offer in Australia.

Pinky remembers the telephone interview that led to her current job and one particular question worried her. The recruitment agency asked Pinky whether she would be happy to work in an 'isolated' location in Australia. One thing she did know about Australia was that it was a very big country! That meant that 'isolated' could mean working anywhere! It could mean working in the red centre of Australia or in the tropical north of Darwin. Again, she knew nothing of the geography involved and the possibilities of where she would end up.

Another challenge on the horizon was that the facility that she was being recruited for specialised in dementia patients, an area that she had absolutely no experience in. However, when the facility agreed to sponsor her migration, Pinky embraced this new set of challenges—a new clinical area; an unfamiliar and vast location; and the need to start again. When Pinky secured the job, her first question was: *"are there any other Filipinos working in the facility?"*.

Being 'here' With (Part of) the Family .

Pinky arrived in Australia in September 2011 under a temporary visa arrangement: the now defunct 457 visa, sponsored by a well-established dementia facility located south of Sydney at the edge of a spectacular area of bushland. The serenity of the surroundings was in deep contrast to what was happening within the buildings. Many of the residents with advanced dementia at the facility had significant behavioural issues that other facilities had been unable to cope with. There was a lot to learn in this unfamiliar clinical environment. Her ability to communicate with other members of staff presented a number of problems because different names were used for different medications and medical procedures than those with which she was familiar. Understanding the nuances of Australian accents was also hard for Pinky and local colleagues and residents also had difficulties understanding her accent. At times she experienced negative comments about not being trained in Australia that upset her, but she also felt that these comments made her work harder than everyone else. Her view was *"I'm not here to please them. I'm here for my family."*

In time, Pinky did have the opportunity to bring her children out to live with her after many years of separation. She applied for Australian residency so that her children could attend school without incurring significant costs. She had been reunited with at least part of her family.

Different personalities deal with similar situations differently. For Pinky there was a realisation early in life that she may not be able to do everything 'perfectly', but she also had enormous faith that she would do her best. Her mantra in any situation remains: *"Okay it's not going to be perfect. It's not going to be easy. But I will just do my best, keep on trying; keep on trying. At the end of the day I am just thinking I'm lucky that I'm here."*

But there was little to do with luck and a lot to do with hard work and sacrifice. Pinky has been living outside of the Philippines for over seven years and during that time has only seen her children intermittently. Many Filipino families, particularly those who have grown up in relatively poor areas where the prospect of education and employment are small, have gone through similar processes. Pinky has had limited opportunity to be with her husband, and the strain this has put on their relationship has intensified over time. She will return home for six weeks over Christmas later in the year and for her son's birthday, however the prospect of her husband joining her to live permanently with her in Sydney slowly fades. His business in the Philippines is doing very well and she knows he would struggle to get work in Australia. Pinky is visibly upset by the separation:

> *I would love him to be here for the sake of the family being together. But I cannot force him. I'm not even sure if he will find a good work or a*

good job that he will be satisfied with. It must be coming from him that he wants to come here. But that hasn't happened.

Separation deepens over time. Pinky knows his business is prospering and his family is becoming more embedded in local politics. Since Pinky has been working in New Zealand and Australia, her husband has developed deeper networks and these networks are increasingly harder to sever. She knows that he would not be able to start again in a new country or turn his back on his family's economic and political affiliations.

While still quite young, Pinky is almost resigned to the fact that she may not be reunited with her husband until she retires. However, what will happen to her children and their educational opportunities? Her son is only ten years old, so the potential for the whole family to be together seems many years away. The repercussions of her forcing this situation and bringing the family together are clear.

I would love for us to be really together, but I don't want to force it. Otherwise if there would be consequences I will be blamed. It's hurting me. It's hurting. It's painful. I don't know what will be the—for us being away physically with—you know we have needs. He has needs. I don't know what will be the outcome of that? But, you know me, I'm just taking it one day at a time. I don't want to pressure myself at the end, what will be the result. What will be the outcome of us not being together? But I don't want to pressure myself at this moment.

Pinky sees the Philippines as her home. When she retires and leaves the nursing profession, she knows that she will return to her home country. Where her children will be at that stage, she does not know. Having attended both school and university here she suspects that the employment options for her daughters will be better in Australia than in the Philippines. Her dream and her aspiration are that her children have more opportunities than she has had, or at least as many as she has had.

Pinky's daughters are already on their way, one with a nursing degree and another with an accounting qualification. Her eyes well up with tears when she talks of her desire for her children to have a 'good life', which for her means an educated life. She is proud of having provided those opportunities for her children. She says:

I'm proud of myself really. It has been a long journey. This is really a good place. This is really a very safe place. I know my kids will have a good future ahead of them.

Pinky is attempting to slow down personally and professionally to take stock of where she is and what she has achieved. Last year she completed a postgraduate certificate in aged care nursing at the Australian College of Nursing as well as completing several short nursing courses. When she reflects on her life, she admits that it has been very stressful studying, working in new clinical areas and establishing herself in two new countries. Being a single mother to three young children has also taken a big toll.

At this moment Pinky feels like she could benefit from a 'rest'. When she initially migrated from the Philippines the intention was for the whole family to migrate together. Along the way her husband's business has prospered and he has become more embedded in his local community, both economically and politically. This means that he keeps postponing the possibility of them being together as a family in Australia. Now, she wonders if he will ever come to live with her and their children in Australia.

Pinky's abiding dream has been to provide her children with a good education. Along the way that has been tough both for her and her family. She tells her daughters the same things she has been telling herself for many years:

> *Okay look at this. You have graduated. You have a job. You have a stable job. You're earning a lot. You have your own car now. You're saving for your future. Look at your classmates back home. They don't have a job. They have graduated but look at them. They have nothing.*

For Pinky the gulf between 'here' and 'back home' can be huge. The sacrifices wear lightly on her young face, but like many before her, Pinky has embraced some wonderful opportunities and made some very big sacrifices over the span of her adult life. Her migration has led to her being separated from her husband and son for much of her son's life. But it has also provided important educational and employment opportunities and helped her create a life for herself and her family that she knew would not be possible in the Philippines. She has in many ways successfully fulfilled some very heartfelt dreams as she builds, and rebuilds, the life around her.

8 Simmi

The Indian Army and Navy
and then Australia

Introduction

Simmi has a quiet, reserved humility that accompanies her small, compact frame. The tranquil surroundings of the aged care and specialist dementia facility located in bushland in the outskirts of Sydney where she currently works is far removed from her military upbringing in India. These beautiful surroundings reflect her appreciation of where she is in her life, despite the daily challenges that a job in an aged care facility may present. Her early determination to be a nurse, contrary to her father's initial wishes that she become a doctor, and her drift back into a military family after she married, seem to follow seamlessly along a rich and highly mobile, but rewarding nursing career.

After nearly ten years living and working in Australia, Simmi is clearly happy with her achievements and alive to the possibilities of more professional and personal opportunities. While the road may not always have been smooth, you get the sense that Simmi is not the type of person that dwells on setbacks. She strikes you as someone that always looks on the positive side of her circumstances and brushes off the darker times in her past. Life (and her upbringing) may have taught her that there is little to be gained from dwelling on the obstacles that present themselves in life, but rather better to spend time focusing on how she, and those around her, can be uplifted by the opportunities that may come along.

Being 'there' in the Wonder of a Sheltered Life

Simmi grew up as a child of the Indian Air Force in India's capital, New Delhi, the political and financial capital and seat of government of India. Growing up in the army villages seemed incredibly glamorous with the well-equipped facilities and plenty of distractions for the children living in the complex, which included Simmi and her younger sister.

The constant moving every two to three years from one part of India to another, did not seem to faze Simmi, as she negotiated new schools, new surroundings and new friends. Her mother grounded the family with each move and protected the two young daughters from the complications and day-to-day logistics that such transience can present. Education and a studious attitude always came first for her mother. Simmi recounted: *"She never wanted us to even participate in any domestic chores because all she wanted us to do was to study and do well in life . . . I think it has paid off [laughs]"*.

Simmi's family had a long history in the military service. Her father was recruited into the Indian Air Force due to his specialisation in communication as a radio technician. His own father had been a Colonel in World War II and military life reached back several generations within the family. Simmi remembers her childhood and formative years as being very secure and happy. Along with her younger sister, she attended local schools although they lived in what could be described as a 'gated' tight-knit community. The army base housed several thousand soldiers, officers and their families and each day the army bus would pick up all of the children to take them to school and deliver them home in the afternoon. The children played together after school, meeting at the army base park in the evening, watching television together and visiting the camp cinema. There were abundant venues within the community including the air force officers' mess, the sailors' mess and bingo and dance hall, swimming pools, squash courts and badminton courts. The facilities were far and above what many neighbouring Indian families might enjoy or as Simmi noted: *"luxurious . . . it's like a world in itself"*, isolated from the families who lived in less fortunate conditions in the surrounding suburbs.

Simmi remembers that she had everything that she wanted right at her door-step. The future was an open field. She reflected that when she was growing up, she only ever thought about becoming a doctor: *"I always had that passion that I have to go into medicine, I have to be a doctor, I have to make my parents proud."* The academic scores that she received at school made medicine a plausible option. As a young 12-year-old girl Simmi clearly recognised that academic achievements gave her more career options, but also made her parents extremely happy and proud. But rather than feeling parental pressure to be academic, Simmi felt that her parents concern reflected their own hard-earned achievement and their desire for her to do well and live a happy life. Having a profession was an important part of this dream.

Competition at school was expected:

> *when I was in school there was a lot of competition, we were very competitive about the marks we were getting. Even though we were close friends we always wanted to be better than the other people academically. I think I was very competitive from the very beginning.*

At around the age of 17 or 18, Simmi followed through her plan to enter the medical profession and sat both the armed forces medical test and armed forces medical nurses test. As with other students across India at the time, she sat these tests on the same day and waited anxiously for the results. Her results came through and Simmi was ecstatic. While she had failed the medical test, she had passed the nursing test. Her father was disappointed with the results. Simmi told her father: *"there's no harm, this is the same thing. Dad said 'no, just wait for one more year, you're very young, maybe next time you will pass the doctors test, with your intelligence you will do it'"*. Simmi refused to wait and relished the opportunity to join the army ranks and to finally wear the uniform. The excitement of starting a new chapter in her life made her impatient. She packed her bags and got measured up for her new uniform, eager to follow in her father's footsteps.

Being able to follow your own career wishes is not guaranteed in all Indian families. Simmi's parents were quite progressive in that way. Her mother was supportive of her desire to follow her own occupational choices and her father was proud that she followed him into the armed forces. He accompanied her to the interview, to her medical checks and transported her to her first training session.

Simmi was clearly excited and challenged by the army training and thought her new job was very glamorous. Even today, decades later, she still feels that the Army, the Navy and Air Force retain considerable glamour in terms of the lifestyle that can be enjoyed. She thought there was a: *"kind of protected life and the glamour that you see in the armed forces and the facilities that we get, it's a struggle for civilians to get those . . . probably that made me marry a naval officer [laughs]"*.

During this period, Simmi was living with her parents in Punjab, a state in North India because her father was posted to Amritsar, the city of the Golden Temple. While training, her posting took her to the southern state of Kerala. It was in this state and in the city of Ernakulam, the eastern, mainland portion of the city of Kochi in central Kerala, that Simmi received three years of training on an Indian naval hospital ship, 'Sanjivani'. The hospital was commissioned in 1958 to service the naval community and ex-servicemen in the region and the medical teams there performed a variety of functions including disaster relief efforts both within and outside India.

These years in training were some of the best years of Simmi's life and she has remained in contact with the other nurses she met while she was training there. Simmi was also very successful. She came dux of her year in all three years while she was training in Ernakulam and during the first and third year, she received the chief of staff's role trophy and three gold medals for her achievements. Simmi had obviously found her niche and she had made her parents very proud.

Being ' in-between': Within India

The successes Simmi had achieved in Kerala were to serve her well in her later attempt to migrate to Australia, but this was not on her mind at the time. She was accustomed to studying hard, so these achievements were the natural outcome of hard work. After Simmi had qualified in 1989 she was commissioned into the armed forces for nine months as a midwife. In 1991 she was posted to an army hospital at Bathinda, a town in Punjab, North India. Here she would meet her future husband who came from Chandigarh, about three hours' drive from Bathinda.

A close friend, whom Simmi trained in Kerala, knew a budding young lieutenant in the Navy whom she had also met while training. When he asked the mutual friend where Simmi was, she said, *"she's right here, not very far away"*, to which he replied, *"I want to meet her"*. The mutual friend was accustomed to Simmi's shyness so she did not tell her that he was very keen on her because she knew that if she did, Simmi would avoid him. As Simmi reflects, she realised now how her friend had orchestrated a meeting knowing that she would have to make up a story to make the meeting happen.

In India it is very important that families meet prospective husbands and wives early in any courtship. In this case, Simmi's future husband asked several of her friends to meet his family to make sure she didn't think that the gathering represented any formal viewing for his parents of her as a prospective bride.

When he proposed to her three days later, she was a little shocked. *"I actually cried at that time because I didn't see it coming."* Being very practical about these things, Simmi wondered how an army and navy union might work. She thought about it overnight and spoke with her mutual friend whose advice went something like this: *He doesn't smoke, he doesn't drink, he doesn't have any bad habits, he's a budding officer and you know Simmi, you two are very alike and I'm telling you, you will do very well together.*

Before Simmi could make any decision, she knew she needed to discuss this union with her parents and more importantly, her parents must meet her future husband's parents. Like many Indian women, Simmi would not go against her parents' wishes. If they disagreed with the coupling, then Simmi would have to refuse the wedding proposal. Again, practicality came to the fore: *"Whatever my parents say is what I'm going to do because I'm not in love with you or anything like that"*. She rationalised this approach on the basis that she hardly knew this man.

Luckily Simmi's parents liked him and his family, and Simmi became engaged in March 1991 with an expectation that the couple would marry that year. However, before the wedding could take place, Simmi's mother unexpectedly died of a heart attack. This tragedy came completely out of the blue. While the sadness was all-consuming, Simmi's wedding was postponed to the following year, April 1992.

Another tragedy soon followed when her husband's aunt faced surgery for advanced breast cancer the day after the wedding. This did not seem like a time for celebration. A simple temple wedding ceremony took place with no accompanying dowry. After the ceremony, 24-year-old Simmi walked into her new house with a suitcase containing all of her worldly possessions, including clothes and pieces of jewellery. A new stage of her life was about to begin.

Combining Army and Navy life was not as easy as Simmi had imagined. She was accustomed to a military life, but Navy life relies on proximity to a coastline while Army life moves from one corner of the country to another. These logistical difficulties created challenges for the newlyweds, so Simmi decided to leave the Army and move into Navy life.

As newlyweds, there was the continual moving and the continual separation as her husband took up posts in Chennai, Visakhapatnam, Kerala and Mumbai.

Uncharacteristically for a Navy man, Simmi's husband did not drink alcohol. The promotions, and the celebrations of higher 'ranks' and 'stripes' were regularly accompanied by milk rather than alcohol. Their plans during the early stages of marriage were to enjoy this time together, getting to know each other and to acclimatise to the Naval lifestyle. The birth of their son followed in 1992 and then their daughter arrived several years later. While happy, Simmi yearned for a more professional focus so she completed her Bachelor of Science in Nursing from Indira Gandhi Open University.

Simmi knew that she was a good nurse. She also knew, however, that at that precise time in her life she needed to be a good mother too. So, she focused her attention on raising her children while also keeping one eye on her education *"so that tomorrow when I want to pick up a job it's going to be very easy"*.

The family continued to relocate for work purposes settling in different posts—from Bombay to Visakhapatnam and from Visakhapatnam to Kochi, back to where she had undertaken her training. Her husband's regular absence was something she shared with the other naval wives. But the women always made sure they were helping each other. As Simmi noted: *"because all the husbands are gone, all the ships have gone so we say bye to all ships and we welcome all ships when they come back. When they are not here, we would actually have parties amongst ourselves"*.

There was a change of direction though. Returning to Delhi in 2001 after her first child was born, Simmi had the opportunity to work with a multinational company that recruited nurses to work in the US and Canada. It was at this point that Simmi began to ask herself: *"how can we make our life even better than what we are doing at the moment? These thoughts would appear and disappear. Because she was preparing others to go to America, she thought why don't I try for myself?"*.

Around this same period of time, one of her friends contacted her to tell her there had been an advertisement placed to recruit Indian nurses to work in Australia. Simmi says, *"So, I thought okay, that's good, let's try. There's no harm"*.

In late 2004, she passed her language tests, completed her paperwork, her audio-conferencing interview with Uniting Care, Australia and was then offered a job. She signed the contract while in India and had a full-time job offer starting July 2005. The whole process from beginning to end took no more than four months. Before she knew it, Simmi and her family, had relocated, but this time, far away to Australia.

Being 'here'

> To begin with, Simmi arrived in Melbourne in February 2005, leaving her young children and her husband behind in India. Her thoughts were: *I can't really believe it! How did this happen? It looked as if God has pushed me, 'Simmi there's an opportunity you must take it'. Just everything fell into place.*

Simmi arrived with a group of 21 other Indian nurses who had come through the same recruitment agent, all of them intending to study at Melbourne's La Trobe University. Between February and July that year the group completed an advanced diploma in general nursing and when they graduated, most travelled north after securing different jobs in various locations in Sydney. Simmi went to a Uniting Care facility in Peakhurst, Sydney as a registered nurse and her agent helped her to convert her student visa to a 457 sponsored work visa.

This new position in aged care, sparked a new interest for Simmi. This occupational speciality was a little novel for Simmi because in India aged care is not the developed industry that it is in Australia. As in many other countries outside Australia, Indian families are more likely to care for a sick or elderly relative within their own homes and without the support of hospitals and medical staff.

Simmi was drawn into the specialty of aged care through her personal experiences of watching her own parents age with limited family support. Simmi felt helpless and far away from her own mother when she unexpectedly died and she felt unable to care for her father when he also fell ill some years later. Both of these events crystallised in Simmi's consciousness that she needed to work in aged care to look after those who had limited family nearby.

With Simmi in Australia, her husband waited for his release from the Indian Navy. After ten months of separation, her husband and their two children, joined her in Australia in 2005. Simmi knew that her husband had made considerable sacrifices too, foregoing a fulfilling career in the Navy and leaving two years short of receiving a full pension, but as Simmi reflects: *"no amount of money is going to compensate for a family living together. So, if we have to struggle, we're going to struggle together"*.

The path for a migrant partner is never easy as the possibility of securing comparable work is even harder than it is for the principal migrant. Having worked in the Navy also represented a liability in a new country as access to security sovereign secrets means that securing a job in the defence force in a foreign nation is impossible. However, Simmi's husband's agreeable personality meant that a job in sales would come easily.

Over the years, the family dynamic had changed. Simmi's husband had moved into unknown occupational territory to find work, and the work that he did find was accorded a much lower status and wage than he was accustomed to in the Indian Navy. It was like being back at square one! As Simmi notes, migration rarely involves the agreement of one decision-maker:

> *Somebody who didn't know anything about sales, has sailed ships all his life, had never ironed clothes, had never done any household jobs, here helps me to do everything and irons the clothes as well, because we share workload. We don't have any domestic help here anymore [laughs]. Yeah, he is wonderful. From day one he was a wonderful husband. Otherwise I would not be here. If he put his foot down, I wouldn't be here.*

Since living in Sydney, Simmi has moved between jobs that have involved night shifts while raising young children; completing a Master's degree in Health at the University of Wollongong, graduating with distinction. Doing this allowed her to develop a greater expertise in health, leadership and management which has helped her to fulfil her aim of moving into a management role. She then took a secondment at an aged care facility specialising in dementia patient care in July 2012 where she remains today.

An important part of Simmi's job now at the aged care facility is to ensure the centre gives quality care to all of the dementia residents. The job of organising family case conferences is an important way that Simmi can get a sense of what palliative approach the resident and their family will take. These patients are some of the most challenging patients that nurses need to manage. Like all nursing, there are good days and bad days. As she reflects:

> *I won't say every day is a good day. But when you take a commitment to look after people with dementia, we have to always consider that the care we are going to extend to a person with dementia has to be extended to their family too. We can't separate a family from the resident. So, we are actually looking after the entire family. To be able to do that we have to understand their perspective. What is their unique story?*

The case conferences are therefore a very important part of getting to know who the patient is behind that mask of dementia. It requires quiet and considered time with patients to understand their individual needs and anxieties. Simmi must find out from the family what the personality of the patient was like before the onset of the disease, what their unique story is and how the other family members influenced their life; what they might be concerned about. She spends some time thinking about what she would do if she were walking in their shoes. These family conferences help Simmi take unbiased and compassionate decisions about patients' needs that put them at the centre of the care plan.

Of course, dementia is a unique disease. Unlike other nursing specialities it requires extreme patience and strategy because many residents have extremely challenging behavioural issues that no other facility can cope with. Many patients display feelings of physical aggression, agitation, and many are also at risk of putting themselves in harm.

Simmi reflects that the rewards of working in this environment relate to her ability to give comfort to patients who deserve this support at this stage of their life. The facility where she works is their home. She wants to ensure that the last few years of their lives are worthwhile to them and their family members. Most importantly, she wants to ensure that she is able to provide a resident *"a good death, a dignified, good death"*. Perhaps she is drawing back to her own parents. She wants to ensure that these patients experience the kind of death that is better than the one that she feels her parents had faced.

Looking Ahead

Right now, at this moment, Simmi feels that she and her family are very well settled. But of course, there is always the future challenge that she sees around the corner. She thinks back over her life and reflects that it has not been particularly difficult. But she does think that as a migrant it has been important for her to prove herself more than others might have had to due to her migrant status. She feels that she has had to strive a little harder to do her best because she did not want people to say: *"Oh my God, who did I get? Who brought this Indian nurse in?"*.

After working for nearly a decade in Australia, Simmi feels that she is now *Indo-Australian*. She has always had a secular approach to life and displays many gods in her home. She advises her children to practise whatever religion they choose to follow. She celebrates many Indian festivals, has many Indian friends who she comes together with to celebrate festivals so as to ensure that her children do not forget their Indian cultural heritage. But with regards to the religious and spiritual issue: *"no, everybody can do what they want"*.

Food is an entirely different matter. Simmi is a self-proclaimed hard-core Indian vegetarian. Unfortunately, her husband and children are not! And to accommodate all tastes, Simmi makes several meals to appeal to all family members. Given that her mother would never let her cook growing up (she was encouraged to study) Simmi follows popular television cooking shows like 'My Kitchen Rules' closely to pick up new recipes, *"but I'll always make sure that I have my Indian vegetarian for myself in the fridge!"*.

In terms of looking at what the future might hold, Simmi often defaults to the prospect of further study, but when prodded more deeply, she reflects: *"I think I'm doing very well. I'm settled, we have our house, we've got beautiful pets, kids are doing well. Shall I say . . . enjoy the life and just do no more study, just now I want to see my kids settle."*

When Simmi reflects over the entirety of her life, she concludes: *"I'm actually good now"*. However, I suspect that Simmi would probably always say that. She has never been the kind of person to make others aware that things were anything but 'good'.

9 Conclusion

Introduction

Patterns of global migration within a global context are often analysed by scrutinising variations in the number of people who cross national borders; the countries from which they leave and to which they settle; and the policies that allow this mobility to take place. Such statistical and policy analysis shows that over the past several decades migration trends have changed dramatically. In particular, female migration has been increasing with skilled women from more diverse countries of origin undertaking this journey (Kofman and Raghuram, 2009; Boucher, 2015; Donato and Gabbacia, 2015).

Our earlier review of the literature highlighted that for many decades now, skilled women, such as nurses, had either explicitly or unconsciously used 'their migrant cap as their passport' to travel and work outside of their home countries, either hopping from country to country or leaving to settle for work abroad. While this is not new, the trend has continued apace due to state support for employer-sponsored and demand-driven migration over the past few decades within Australia and in many other countries whose healthcare sector relies on overseas-qualified nurses. These, and other factors, have accelerated and changed the nature and profile of global mobility significantly.

The state, as potentially both an employer and a legislator of migration policy, represents a dominant player shaping the work and the life opportunities of migrant nurses. Further, given the increasingly explicitly commercial nature and tone of migration, there is an increased role for commercial recruitment agencies and intermediaries that service the mobility of nurses and other workers (Abella, 2004; Xiang, 2012; Groutsis et al., 2015; van den Broek et al., 2015). As such, nurses' mobility and careers have been significantly influenced and regulated by the vagaries of organisational, industrial and institutional actors and the market.

However, there are other important factors at play here around gender, familial and individual aspiration, hopes, dreams and opportunity seeking. For example, gendered patterns of migration reflect the different ways that men and women experience and interact with migration policies (Piper, 2006). The sexual segregation of the workforce in Australia, as in many other countries, means that occupational selectivity of national migration policy results in a highly gendered migration process. For example, men have tended to dominate occupational fields such as engineering and information communication technologies, while women have dominated in fields such as health care, social services and education. Therefore, when governments prioritise the entry of a particular visa category and occupational field, they also unavoidably prioritise the entry of either women or men. These factors reflect how migration policy is inextricably linked to the gendering of work as women and men seek, and are funnelled into, different jobs offered in different parts of the world.

Having an understanding of how institutions and organisations regulate and thus 'gender' nurse migration is therefore important in contextualising individual decisions about nurse mobility (Tams and Arthur, 2010; Xu and Zhang, 2005). While employment is closely determined by visa or migration status, mobility plans may be highly strategised or deeply serendipitous as noted in the preceding stories! Individual agency, which shapes opportunity, is highly contextual. For example, one nurse might intend to embark on a temporary working holiday with every intention of returning to her home country, while another may be fleeing war and conflict, poor employment prospects or difficult political, economic or family circumstances that make plans to return to their home country highly complex. While there are a variety of circumstances that prompt these individual journeys, personal family relations and professional expectations have a huge influence on the directions and decisions these women make (Carling, 2005; De Haas, 2014).

As Louise Ryan highlights, migration is also a highly charged emotional journey that often involves feelings of loneliness and homesickness (2008). While in many respects migration represents a positive move that increases personal and professional opportunity, there is also usually an element of constraint or even resignation. There are many feelings that are torn and contradictory. As we see in the case of Mei and Jo from China and Korea particularly, there is a sense that migration was a definite plan that was thought through early in their lives and explicitly carried out to achieve professional and personal opportunity. For Pinky however, there seemed an inevitability that her migration from the Philippines would be a (temporary) means to ensure that her three children would have a better life and education than she had experienced up until now. Much like Pinky, Simmi also saw her journey here as one of ensuring a better life for her and her family. For Sheila, who left the UK after many years of nursing experience, the choices were much more lifestyle orientated, while for Cynthia there was a strange tension between lifestyle, escape and new adventure.

Given the diversity in the experiences of migrant nurses, it is impossible to generalise about the many circuits of transnational migration that take place in nursing and other migration routeways—into a new country and into a new occupational context. It is relatively safe to say however that the women whose stories are included in this book have, relatively speaking, had very positive experiences. None of the six women here were overtly forced to flee war-torn conflicts or violent personal circumstances, and most did not grow up in the poorest families in their societies. Of course, there are many nurses who have experienced much more difficult, dangerous and complex circumstances than those included in this book.

The women included in this book all accepted the offer of work in the Australian healthcare sector. In general, their stories are not dramatic or extraordinary to the outside observer. However, it is exactly these stories that show us how migrant nurses, working and caring for us in our local hospitals, have negotiated around many personal and professional challenges. These challenges might have arisen from the differences in culture and language; loneliness and isolation, or just the mundane challenges that many face balancing life and work: that is, parents, partners, children, colleagues and employers (Ryan, 2008; George, 2005). These challenges may not be highly visible or even clearly articulated, but they are an ever-present daily reality for many migrants living and working.

Why This Book was Written

The aim of this book was to offer an alternative and complementary perspective to the existing literature on migrant nurses. It was intended to allow individual nurses' personal migration stories to take precedence over these broader political, economic and labour-market priorities that traditionally dominate analysis.

The purpose of the book was to unravel the 'lived experience' of migration at an individual level. It is hoped that their experiences resonate with many of us, as both workers and as citizens who live in a country where our health and well-being have come to rely heavily on the willingness and enthusiasm of the women who shared their stories with us.

While this account does not seek to romanticise these women's lives, or build a fairy tale around their migration stories, it does aim to illuminate what compelled them to leave their homes and join a migrant healthcare workforce that has now reached unparalleled levels. Although we focus on the stories of women who have migrated to Australia through their nursing career, many of the experiences and feelings we learn about here apply to all migrant workers.

The personal and professional expectations and experiences, which are often internalised and left unsaid, show us that the people behind the statistics share deep courage, and optimism but also trepidation and self-doubt, as they undertake their journey, often alone. Their stories show us that migration is not an act undertaken lightly or something that, once done, is finished and then forgotten. The situations of the women in this book change over time, however, there always seems to be a lingering connection to the country where they are born, and the countries to which they move to live. This book grants a valuable insight into these nurses' profession, their dedication and the challenges and fears they and others like them, face. The basic rationale for this book is simply that we should understand a lot more about the women who make a living helping to nurse us, our families and our friends away from sickness and into health.

How This Book was Written

A life can be told and understood in a variety of different ways. We chose to collect the life stories of six nurses we got to know through interviews that illuminated their lives and particularly their careers. As they spoke about their journeys between one country to another it became clear that many of the women had experienced considerable fragmentation and vulnerability over their life.

There was a strong reflection on the part of these women about the countries and families that they had left behind and the journey they took to arrive here. The sense that there was a life they left behind turned into our first theme we presented as Being 'there'. This section reflected the feeling that each participant in this book had about her early life growing up in her home country with her family and friends during formative years. The feelings expressed in this section of each woman's life tells us something about why they chose, or gravitated towards, the nursing profession. We also come to understand how the decision to move away from their roots emerges. The section retells the extraordinary dreams of ordinary people, many of whom consider their work more as a calling than just a job (Terkel, 1974, xxix).

For example, from an early age many were drawn to the nursing profession because they felt a strong need to help others, or because their mother or another relative had also trained as a nurse. The mobility attached to the profession was also a strong attraction for some, such as Mei who knew she would travel overseas from a very early age to seek professional opportunity. For Sheila however, following in her mother's footsteps was more important than travel, with her itchy feet not taking her abroad for work until much later in her career. Pinky was never in any doubt that she would take up a nursing career. All of the nurses included here were close to family and while relatively practical about the need to migrate, it was clear that this period growing up with family in familiar surroundings still links closely to the deep sense of connection to 'home' and belonging that they still feel to this day.

The second period of 'Being in-between' should not give the impression that this was a chronological period of time. It refers to a time in their lives when they were experimenting with different possibilities in terms of where and how they would live. This was a period when these women were aware that they needed to move away from all that they knew so they could test out their nursing qualifications in different professional settings. For some, such as Jo, this meant travelling and working in several countries where she knew she would not settle permanently, such as the United Arab Emirates.

The final section titled 'Being here' again does not infer that these women had arrived at their final destination. It merely recognises that they have found themselves living here in Australia where their story is being told. For most of the women, there were definitely challenges that needed to be faced, however there was also a feeling of satisfaction about where they had come to and a relative feeling of having established security both personally and professionally—well, for most.

Taking this three-phase approach allowed us to understand how these women articulated an everyday 'lived' sense of why they joined the profession as young women and what compelled them to seek new lives away from their families and friends. We wanted to give them a platform from which to tell their own stories without over-interpretation, speculation or further analysis. We wanted these women to share a wider humanity that underscored the opportunities and challenges they faced with as wide an audience as possible.

Retelling Women, Work and Migration

All the women in this book tell a story that is both public and private, political and social, collective and individual. They highlight how workers shape, and are shaped by, the industry they work in, the country context and the associated cultural, social, political, economic and institutional arrangement; and the broader trends in migration that envelop them. Their stories provide a crucial human element that helps us to understand their personal endeavours in an industry that would be unable to function without them.

While work means different things to different people, it has significant meaning in all of our lives. Many of us may look back on our lives and our work and wonder where and how we got to where we are now. As a young woman Jo dreamed of being a lawyer or a teacher and saw herself migrating to America. But life took Jo into different directions both occupationally and geographically—from Seoul, to Saudi Arabia and then to Australia.

There is considerable optimism amongst all of the women in these pages about the life they have forged in Australia, however they have also experienced challenging times. Recent mapping projects surveying 2,300 Australian respondents indicate that 81% of skilled migrants arriving in Australia between 2000–2010 were satisfied with their life here, however four out of ten immigrants surveyed from non-English-speaking backgrounds reported 'relatively high' levels of discrimination on the basis of skin colour, ethnic origin, or religion. This was more than double the average of the total migrants surveyed (Markus, 2014). As such, there are obvious high and low points that every migrant faces as they integrate into new countries and new cultures.

Conclusion

In some respects, many of the women here have unique stories. In other ways their experiences have many common threads. Many faced economic challenges as they pursued their nursing careers and emotional challenges as they often forged a life alone in a new country. These are very familiar stories that resonate with many migrants who leave a country and a family behind to join new cultures, societies and workplaces while still maintaining very strong emotional and financial links to their home countries.

If we haven't taken that step to migrate ourselves, or know someone intimately who has, it may be hard to fully understand what that journey might feel like. For many of us the migration 'story' is often digested in the form of numbers or faceless figures. Or they have been digested through political debates that tell us very little about the individuals that make these journeys and what they contribute when they arrive. However, these women are more than numbers and more than just fodder for political debates. They are individuals who have led unique and colourful lives. They may one day nurse us, or members of our families, back to health. We should not underestimate their contribution and we gain much by taking the time to think about the memories and dreams they have that brought them here, that have shaped their past and build their tomorrow. Only then can we fully understand their work that remains central to our individual and our nation's collective health and well-being.

References

Abella, M. I. (2004). The role of recruiters in labor migration. In Douglas S. Massey and J. Edward Taylor (Eds.), *International Migration: Prospects and Policies in a Global Market* (pp. 201–211). Oxford: Oxford University Press.

Boucher, A. (2015). *Gender, Migration and the Global Race for Talent.* Manchester: Manchester University Press.

Carling, J. (2005). Gender dimensions of international migration. *Global migration perspectives, 35*, 1–26.

De Haas, H. (2014). *Migration Theory: Quo Vadas?* International Migration Institute, Working Paper Series, Paper 100, November.

Donato, K. M. and Gabbacia, D. (2015). *Gender and International Migration.* Russell Sage Foundation.

George, S. M. (2005). *When Women Come First: Gender and Class in Transnational Migration.* Berkeley: University of California Press.

Groutsis, D., van den Broek, D., and Harvey, W. S. (2015). Transformations in network governance: The case of migration intermediaries. *Journal of Ethnic and Migration Studies,* 41(10), 1558–1576.

Kofman, E. and Raghuram, P. (2009). *Skilled Female Labour Migration.* Policy Brief, Focus Migration, No. 13, April.

Markus, A. (2014). *Mapping Social Cohesion: The Scanlon Foundation Surveys Recent Arrivals Report 2013.*

Piper, N. (2006). Gendering the politics of migration. *International Migration Review,* 40(1), 133–164.

Ryan, L. (2008). Navigating the emotional terrain of families "here" and "there": Women, migration and the management of emotions. *Journal of Intercultural Studies,* 29(3), 299–313.

Tams, S., & Arthur, M. B. (2010). New directions for boundaryless careers: Agency and interdependence in a changing world. *Journal of Organizational Behavior, 31*(5), 629–646.

Terkel, S. (1974). *Working: People Talk About What They Do All Day and How They Feel About What They Do.* New York: Pantheon/Random House.

van den Broek, D., Harvey, W. S., and Groutsis, D. (2015, September). Commercial migration intermediaries and the segmentation of skilled migrant employment. *Work, Employment and Society.* http://doi.org/10.1177/0950017015594969

Xiang, B. (2012). Predatory princes and princely peddlers: The state and international labour migration intermediaries in China. *Pacific Affairs,* 85(1), 47–68.

Xu, Y. and Zhang J. (2005). One Size Doesn't Fit All: Ethics of international nurse recruitmentfrom the conceptual framework of Stakeholder Interests, *Nurse Ethics, 12,* 571–581.

Index

Printed in the United States
by Baker & Taylor Publisher Services